T0277259

Cambridge Elements

Elements in Magic
edited by
Marion Gibson
University of Exeter

THE WAR ON WITCHCRAFT

Andrew Dickson White, George Lincoln Burr, and the Origins of Witchcraft Historiography

Jan Machielsen
Cardiff University

CAMBRIDGE
UNIVERSITY PRESS

University Printing House, Cambridge CB2 8BS, United Kingdom

One Liberty Plaza, 20th Floor, New York, NY 10006, USA

477 Williamstown Road, Port Melbourne, VIC 3207, Australia

314–321, 3rd Floor, Plot 3, Splendor Forum, Jasola District Centre,
New Delhi – 110025, India

103 Penang Road, #05–06/07, Visioncrest Commercial, Singapore 238467

Cambridge University Press is part of the University of Cambridge.

It furthers the University's mission by disseminating knowledge in the pursuit of
education, learning, and research at the highest international levels of excellence.

www.cambridge.org
Information on this title: www.cambridge.org/9781108948746
DOI: 10.1017/9781108953313

First published 2021

A catalogue record for this publication is available from the British Library.

ISBN 978-1-108-94874-6 Paperback
ISSN 2732-4087 (online)
ISSN 2732-4079 (print)

The War on Witchcraft

Andrew Dickson White, George Lincoln Burr, and the Origins of Witchcraft Historiography

Elements in Magic

DOI: 10.1017/9781108953313
First published online: June 2021

Jan Machielsen
Cardiff University
Author for correspondence: Jan Machielsen, machielsenj@cardiff.ac.uk

Abstract: Historians of the early modern witch-hunt often begin histories of their field with the theories propounded by Margaret Murray and Montague Summers in the 1920s. They overlook the lasting impact of nineteenth-century scholarship, in particular the contributions by two American historians: Andrew Dickson White (1832–1918) and George Lincoln Burr (1857–1938). Study of their work and scholarly personae contributes to our understanding of the deeply embedded popular understanding of the witch-hunt as representing an irrational past in opposition to an enlightened present. Yet the men's relationship with each other, and with witchcraft sceptics – the heroes of their studies – also demonstrates how their writings were part of a larger war against 'unreason'. This Element thus lays bare the ways scholarly masculinity helped shape witchcraft historiography, a field of study often seen as dominated by feminist scholarship. Such meditation on past practice may foster reflection on contemporary models of history writing.

Keywords: witchcraft historiography, history of science, Andrew Dickson White, George Lincoln Burr, masculinity

ISBNs: 9781108948746 (PB), 9781108953313 (OC)
ISSNs: 2732-4087 (online), 2732-4079 (print)

Contents

1 'Ding! Dong! The Witch is Dead'

From the outset writing witchcraft history was about making witchcraft *history*. When scholars during the early eighteenth century began to reflect on the history of the European witch-hunt they did so with the explicit aim of banishing witchcraft to the past. The historicizing practices of these sceptics have generally been overlooked, but they are the inevitable companion of the other, better-known strategy of presenting witchcraft beliefs solely as the preserve of the credulous multitude.[1] These two strategies come together in a work often regarded as the first history of the witch-hunt, at least for England: Francis Hutchinson's 1718 *An Historical Essay Concerning Witchcraft*.[2] The sceptical minister of Bury St Edmunds and 'a Whig on his way up' denounced 'the credulous Multitude … ever … ready to try their Tricks and swim the old Women', while also marking the time since England's last witchcraft execution – 'thirty five Years last past' – and the nation's reputation as 'the first in these latter Ages that clear'd it self of such Superstitions'.[3] Two centuries later Hutchinson's victory appeared so decisive that Wallace Notestein felt comfortable ending his own 1911 study of witchcraft in England with the publication of this 'final and deadly blow at the dying superstition'.[4] The end of witchcraft was history's triumph, or so it seemed. (Figure 1 offers a striking contemporary illustration of the sceptics' heroic self-regard.)

This attitude has endured for a surprisingly long time. In his 1997 study Ian Bostridge still considered Hutchinson's reply to be 'the last word in the witchcraft debate, a masterpiece of humane rationalism'.[5] Yet Bostridge also recovers Hutchinson's anxieties about the timing of the work's publication and its possible reception, and he points out the artificiality of the main argument: the

---

[1] On this 'historicizing' point, see my review of Hunter, *The Decline of Magic*, and the author's response: Machielsen, 'Review of "The Decline of Magic"'.

[2] See e.g. Gaskill, 'The Pursuit of Reality', p. 1069. Gaskill presents Christian Thomasius's 1701 *De crimine magiae* as the 'first history of witchcraft' but there is nothing overtly historical about that treatise. A 1712 law dissertation written by Thomasius and defended by one of his students does take a historical perspective: Thomasius, *Disputatio iuris canonici de origine ac progressu processus inquisitorii contra sagas*. Its aim was to prove that the demonic pact was not more than 600 years old. The claim overlooks the use of the past by authors defending the reality of witchcraft. Hutchinson was responding to Richard Boulton's 1715 *A Compleat History of Magick, Sorcery, and Witchcraft*. The question as to when Europeans began to see the past as a different country is a contentious one. For instance, Lowenthal, *The Past Is a Foreign Country*, p. 4, dates this moment to 'the late eighteenth century', while Schiffman, *The Birth of the Past*, points to Renaissance humanism.

[3] Hutchinson, *An Historical Essay Concerning Witchcraft*, pp. viii, 49, [xviii]. For this description of Hutchinson, see Bostridge, *Witchcraft and Its Transformations*, p. 144.

[4] Notestein, *A History of Witchcraft in England from 1558 to 1718*, p. vi.

[5] Bostridge, *Witchcraft and Its Transformations*, p. 142. The claim that Hutchinson's book was 'in any serious sense' the last word is repeated on p. 153. For Sneddon's refutation of this claim, see Sneddon, *Witchcraft and Whigs*, pp. 123–5.

Figure 1 Daniel Nikolaus Chodowiecki, 'Christian Thomasius Helps an Elderly Witchcraft Suspect out of Her Prison Cell' (1800). Image Courtesy of the Rijksmuseum, Amsterdam.

1712 trial and conviction of Jane Wenham, which preoccupies a sizeable part of the Whig's treatise, showed that the Witchcraft Act had by no means become a dead letter. (Wenham escaped the noose through a royal pardon.[6]) Both Bostridge and Hutchinson's subsequent biographer, Andrew Sneddon, note Hutchinson's redeployment of age-old sceptical arguments ('old wine ... in the new bottles of the "new science"').[7] Strangely, neither scholar has commented on the *Historical Essay*'s historical packaging, evident not only from the title but also from the extended 'Chronological Table' with which it more or less opens.[8] Yet the historical approach aligned well with Hutchinson's moderation. The *Historical Essay* restricted itself to an examination of past cases of fraud, deception, and mental illness, avoiding the radical and complete rejections of the spirit world put forth by Thomas Hobbes, Balthasar Bekker, and Baruch Spinoza. In private, Hutchinson even offered to change his mind about witchcraft, 'if ever experience doth shew the contrary'.[9] Upon closer examination, then, the historian comes across as timid, especially when compared to the universal certainties professed by the philosophers.

From these unheroic beginnings, historians have for generations worked hard to make witchcraft a thing of the past, even – or perhaps especially – when they knew that witchcraft beliefs (or other forms of apparent irrationality) still surrounded them. Parallels between witchcraft belief and fascism – 'another delusion, not so different in its effects or in its locale from the early witchcraft persecutions' – circulated widely during World War II and its aftermath.[10] The influential works of Hugh Trevor-Roper and Norman Cohn published during the 1960s and 1970s were still written in the shadow of a war in which both men had served as British military officers.[11] For such authors witchcraft was truly dead and buried – it had to be – but there was always the anxious possibility that it might return from the grave in another, albeit related, guise. Even today, a prominent historical survey remains committed to 'annihilat[ing]' witchcraft belief, while the 'decline of magic' narrative is proving be to be nearly as persistent as the beliefs whose death it purports to chart.[12]

---

[6] On the Wenham trial and its contemporary reception, see also Guskin, 'The Context of Witchcraft'.

[7] Sneddon, *Witchcraft and Whigs*, p. 110.

[8] The *Essay*'s second chapter is entitled 'Chronological Table of some Tryals and Executions of supposed Witches and Conjurers, and Imposters'. As Andrew Sneddon pointed out to me, Hutchinson engaged in a great number of historical projects throughout his life. As a young man, Hutchinson's 'historical studies' were directed by his maternal uncle, the ejected Puritan minister Francis Tallents: Sneddon, *Witchcraft and Whigs*, p. 19.

[9] Sneddon, *Witchcraft and Whigs*, p. 122.   [10] Guerlac, 'George Lincoln Burr', p. 152.

[11] Trevor-Roper, 'The European Witch-Craze'; Norman Cohn, *Europe's Inner Demons*.

[12] For a study 'designed' to 'annihilate' fears of witches 'by providing a better understanding of the roots of belief in such a figure and how they developed in a European context', see Hutton, *The*

All that said, the historicizing project has mostly been abandoned. At a time when modernity itself seems in peril, historians have come to reject larger, often sociological frameworks of modernization and disenchantment that underpin the very essence of the 'early modern'.[13] The past two decades have seen a venerable boom in studies of nineteenth and twentieth-century witchcraft beliefs as well as studies of how modern Wiccans have constructed new histories of their own.[14] Instead of the decline of magic, historians study its transformation in new guises and new contexts. Still, while academic history has moved on, this earlier campaign to make witchcraft a relic of the past has proved surprisingly successful. In our lecture theatres, seminar rooms, and Zoom classes we are reaping a past vision of history that our predecessors sowed. Students continue to arrive with views of witchcraft as inherently irrational, superstitious, false, and therefore *obviously* past tense.

The problems with these popular attitudes are manifold. They drip with condescension and paternalism towards the past. They evince no understanding of or interest in the agency and beliefs of those involved in the witch-hunt (including the victims themselves); they simply prescribe better knowledge as a panacea.[15] Ironically, these views unwittingly adhere to the same dichotomy between axiomatically true and false beliefs that structured the belief system they so ostentatiously scorn – dressed up in the same (originally religious) language of superstition that the demonologists once used themselves.[16] The problem with the past was simply a lack of scientific rationalism. Refuting such facile assertions of reason or irrationality is not the principal focus of this study, however. These observations are simply a by-product of this Element's central preoccupation: the ways in which witchcraft beliefs have unthinkingly come to be seen as 'past', long before they actually were. (If, indeed, they are.) In 2006 the classicist Christopher Mackay chose as the motto for his new translation of the *Malleus maleficarum* the well-known line by L. P. Hartley that 'the past is a foreign country: they do things differently there'.[17] While frankly uninspired,

---

Witch, p. 280. For the latest articulation of the decline of magic narrative, see Hunter, *The Decline of Magic*. For the point about magic's endurance, see William Pooley's excellent review of the same volume: Pooley, 'Review of "The Decline of Magic"'.

[13] For modernization, see Walker, 'Modernization', esp. pp. 38–9. For a critique of the 'disenchantment of the world' theory, see Walsham, 'The Reformation and "the Disenchantment of the World" Reassessed'.

[14] See especially Waters, *Cursed Britain*, Pooley, 'Magical Capital', and the collection of essays included in Davies and De Blécourt (eds.), *Witchcraft Continued*.

[15] On the agency of victims of the witch-hunt, the starting points remain Roper, *Oedipus and the Devil* and Willis, *Malevolent Nurture*.

[16] Clark, *Thinking with Demons*; Cameron, *Enchanted Europe*.

[17] Institoris and Sprenger, *Malleus Maleficarum*, ed. Christopher S. Mackay.

the choice also reveals how unreflectively *past* witchcraft has become. Metaphorical uses of witchcraft and witch-hunting are instructive. Labelling judicial investigations 'the greatest witch hunt in American history' not only lays claim to innocent victimhood, the grievance also seeks to discredit and delegitimize.[18] Even politicians who blatantly contravene societal and political norms know that witch-hunting is fundamentally not us. It is what our ancestors did. Only the Middle Ages are used in a similar way. The news media abound in denunciations of terrorist atrocities and other horrors, even poor mobile phone reception, as 'medieval'. Both the time period and the witch persecutions are seen as the very essence of past ignorance that can be used to criticize aspects of the enlightened present. These metaphors create a bridge between the past and present that should not exist. It is no wonder that the witch-hunt is so often wrongly seen as a product of the 'Dark Ages', rather than the early modern period.[19]

Historians in recent years have shown renewed interest in 'presentism': the ways in which the present is anachronistically read into the past and the past is put to use in the present.[20] This study is interested in a form of presentism that at first sight might appear its antithesis: the past as a place of banishment, a Pandora's box containing Europe's inner demons, which should remain closed but always risks being opened. Far from its alter ego, this is presentism on steroids – it articulates a relation between past and present which emphasizes difference, distance, and thus moral superiority, though this is always imperilled and cannot be taken for granted. A comprehensive study of the origins of witchcraft's pastness would be a veritable whistle-stop tour. Beyond the case study to which this Element is devoted, it would pay special attention to the 1691 Salem witch-hunt and examine how, almost from the outset, it became lodged in the American national subconscious.[21] It would most certainly explore the long history of metaphorical witch-hunts and the ways these established a parallel between the past and present. World War II, as already suggested, looms particularly large here, with Nazis in the role of witch-hunters. (In 1945, as part of the tercentenary commemorations of the East Anglia Witch-Hunt, *The Essex Newsman* described Witchfinder General

---

[18] By one count President Trump tweeted the words 'Witch Hunt' more than 300 times: Almond, 'You Think This Is a Witch Hunt, Mr President?'

[19] For the examples and the parallel with witch-hunting, see Falk, *The Light Ages*, p. 5.

[20] See e.g. Welch, 'Presentism and the Renaissance and Early Modern Historian', which notes on p. 247 that for witchcraft historians 'the past is not the beginning of today but often an unrecognizable alien environment, one where walking and talking with demons was the norm, not the exception'. The classic, recently revised study of presentism is Lowenthal, *The Past Is a Foreign Country*.

[21] Gibson, *Witchcraft Myths in American Culture*.

Matthew Hopkins as 'the Himmler of his time'.[22]) Especially important in this regard is Arthur Miller's 1953 play *The Crucible* and its attack on McCarthyism.[23] Its enduring influence can be measured by the fact that one recent scholar, in a botched attempt at reactionary revisionism, has called for historians to return to the *play's* understanding of the Salem witch-hunt: 'if ever there were an instance of "throwing the baby out with the bathwater", the post-1960s historians of witchcraft have produced one'.[24]

No study of popular culture could ever be a linear history, however, and a survey would also include those cross-currents that agitate against the witch-hunt's pastness: for Wiccans and feminists the early modern witch-hunt has been a formative injury, as 'the burning times' or a 'gynocide', with conse-quences for the present and future.[25] Indirectly, however, these foundation myths may still contribute to the narrative that interests us here. By doubling down on the *craze* in 'witch-craze' and amplifying its scale to that of a genuine Holocaust, even these rival understandings of witchcraft history as not-past contribute to popular views of the witch-hunt as the very essence of the irrational past.[26]

While others were certainly more important in disseminating and populariz-ing witchcraft's pastness, the two figures at the centre of this study – Andrew Dickson White (1832–1918) and his student George Lincoln Burr (1857–1938) – were instrumental in its formulation. Indeed, the importance of the two nineteenth-century American historians becomes clearer still if we approach our subject genealogically. Their works mark the first contributions to the history of witchcraft within English-speaking academia – White was the first President of the American Historical Association – and very possibly beyond it. The only work which the two men acknowledged as a precursor to their own, and which devoted a chapter on the witch-hunt, was the *History of the Rise and Influence of the Spirit of Rationalism in Europe* (1865), by the gentleman scholar William Lecky.[27] While witchcraft prosecutions had

---

[22] 'The Witch Hunter', *Essex Newsman*, 27 February 1945. I owe this reference to my dissertation student, Robert Pearce.

[23] Miller's own reflections on writing the play are a good starting point: Arthur Miller, 'Why I Wrote "The Crucible"'.

[24] For this unusual use of Miller's play, see Fels, *Switching Sides*, p. 127.

[25] For introductions to these alternative histories, see Shuck, 'The Myth of the Burning Times'. For 'gynocide', see Daly, *Gyn/Ecology*, p. 198.

[26] On the eighteenth-century origins of the figure of nine million executions and its adoption by pagans, feminists, and even Nazis, see Behringer, 'Neun Millionen Hexen'.

[27] In September 1907, when Henry Charles Lea announced to Burr his plan to resume work on his history of witchcraft, he could still claim that 'so far as I am aware, with the exception of Lecky's brief sketch, there is no work in our language on the subject which has any claim to consider-ation': Philadelphia, University of Pennsylvania, MS Coll. 111: Henry Charles Lea papers, Box 4, Folder 209. Cape May, NJ, 7 September 1907. Unlike White and Burr, however, Lecky never

ended, White and Burr still grappled with the same problem that confronted Hutchinson a century earlier: what to do with a superstitious present that is not yet past? Their solution was to position witchcraft within a wider struggle between scientific investigation and religious dogma. This constitutes a – perhaps *the* – crucial link in the development of modern popular understandings of witchcraft. In this larger – indeed, still ongoing – war between rationalism and superstition, the end of witchcraft prosecutions became a hallmark of the progress already made and proof of an enlightened present. White and Burr were warriors. Their histories cast witchcraft into the past as part of an ongoing war against present-day unreason; that war was by no means won, but witchcraft's pastness demonstrated that, with enough effort, it inevitably would be.

These wider objectives indicate that White and Burr cannot be confined to the history of witchcraft. Indeed, placing White within the context of witchcraft historiography may come as a revelation to some, yet the case for doing so is compelling. Witchcraft books and manuscripts form a central part of the President White Library, many of them purchased by Burr on White's behalf in Europe. Cornell University Library, to whom White bequeathed his books, still possesses one of the world's largest collections of such texts.[28] Yet despite his evident interest in the subject, White himself is principally – perhaps solely – remembered for his contributions to the history of science. His two-volume *A History of the Warfare of Science with Theology in Christendom* (hereafter *Warfare of Science* or simply *Warfare*, 1896) has rarely, if ever, been out of print since its first publication. Unlike witchcraft historians, historians of science have long waged a campaign against *Warfare*. Considered to be the origin of many of the falsehoods surrounding the history of science,[29] the work 'is no longer regarded as even a reliable secondary source for historical study'.[30] As such, historians of science have devoted entire volumes to debunking myths propagated by this book.[31] As this suggests, the emphasis has been on refuting rather than understanding White. He acts principally as a straw figure representing the outmoded 'conflict' thesis which postulated mutual hostility

---

held an academic post. White's presidential address was published in its proceedings and its text can still be found on the American Historical Association website: White, 'On Studies in General History and the History of Civilization'. www.historians.org/about-aha-and-membership/aha-history-and-archives/presidential-addresses/andrew-dickson-white-(1884).

28 The Cornell University Witchcraft Collection contains over 3,000 titles, many of them digitized: 'The Cornell University Witchcraft Collection'.

29 See e.g. the comments in Park, 'That the Medieval Church Prohibited Human Dissection', p. 43, and Harrison, *The Territories of Science and Religion*, p. 172.

30 Russell, 'The Conflict of Science and Religion', p. 10.

31 See Numbers (ed.), *Galileo Goes to Jail*; Numbers and Kampourakis (eds.), *Newton's Apple and Other Myths about Science*.

between science and religion.[32] For all its historiographical importance, therefore, the context in which this seminal work was written has been remarkably little studied, as we shall explore further in section 3. Burr's role in the composition of *Warfare of Science* has gone almost entirely unnoticed.[33]

While historians of science have at least taken cognizance of White, students of the early modern witch-hunt have ignored both men.[34] One reason for this lack of attention to the *longue durée* has been the existence of a truncated narrative that roots the origins of witchcraft historiography in the works published by Montague Summers and, especially, Margaret Murray during the 1920s. Although their interpretations could hardly have been more different from each other, both scholars insisted that witchcraft had in some sense been *real*, in a way that White and Burr, as committed 'rationalists', had not.[35] Murray's 1921 *The Witch-Cult in Western Europe* argued that early modern Europe's witches had been members of a secret pagan fertility cult. Summers, an ostentatious convert to Catholicism, argued that demon worship was real and continued in other (e.g. Communist) guises up to the present.[36] Burr, still alive to rebut these claims, insisted on witchcraft's pastness: 'Mr Summers is still in the Middle Ages ... writing to bring back the days of the *Malleus Maleficarum*'.[37] Murray was similarly charged with seeking to turn back time. It was 300 years since Friedrich Spee's *Cautio criminalis*,

> which did most to convince the world that these confessions ... were but fabrications wrung from them by torture. ... The rational eighteenth century invited yet more thoroughgoing revelations; and now for more than a hundred years Protestant scholars and Catholic, once rivals in credulity, have been disputing instead as to the credit for priority in unmasking the cruel delusion.[38]

---

[32] For criticism of the 'conflict' thesis, see esp. Brooke, *Science and Religion*, pp. 1–68.

[33] The existence of Glenn C. Altschuler's excellent biography of White could have been a reason, but I have found it very little cited by historians of science. The only previous discussion of Burr's role is Bainton, 'His Life', pp. 48–58.

[34] The best (though brief) discussion of White's and Burr's role in witchcraft historiography remains Estes, 'Incarnations of Evil', pp. 136–8. Fudge, 'Traditions and Trajectories', p. 493, mentions Burr only in passing and gives the wrong years both for his birth and his death; Gaskill, 'The Pursuit of Reality', p. 1069, lists Burr only as 'inspired' by the Cologne archivist Joseph Hansen, although many of Burr's publications predated Hansen's famous 1900 work. Burr is entirely absent from the otherwise comprehensive survey by Christa Tuczay, 'The Nineteenth Century'.

[35] On Murray and Summers, see esp. Wood, 'The Reality of Witch Cults Reasserted'.

[36] See, in particular, Summers, *The History of Witchcraft and Demonology*.

[37] Burr, 'A Group of Four Books on Witchcraft and Demonology', p. 491. In his autobiography, Summers expressed delight that 'the vulgarians snapped and snarled': Summers, *The Galanty Show*, p. 157.

[38] Burr, 'Review of *The Witch-Cult in Western Europe*', p. 780.

Burr, in the 1920s, struggled to keep the Pandora's box of the past closed.

When British historians returned to the subject of the early modern witch-hunt in the 1960s, they set their sights on Murray. (It seems that Summers, for all his learning and philological skill, could be ignored as a harmless eccentric.) When, in 1967, Hugh Trevor-Roper published his essay on 'The European Witch-Craze of the Sixteenth and Seventeenth Centuries', he told his readers that 'the fancies of the late Margaret Murray need not detain us. They were justly, if irritably, dismissed by a *real scholar* as "vapid balderdash"'.[39] Keith Thomas's tone was more restrained in his 1971 *Religion and the Decline of Magic*, though he similarly dismissed Murray's work as 'much overrated'.[40] Murray's lasting influence (also on the modern Wicca movement), her tenacious defence of her own work (Thomas praised a contemporary for his 'dignified reply to her staggeringly ungenerous notices of his work'), and her longevity (she optimistically entitled her 1963 autobiography *My First Hundred Years*) help account for the sharpness of these attitudes.[41] While no one has been able to salvage Murray's working methods, the gendered nature of these criticisms is hard to miss and has been called out.[42] Both Murray and Summers were also easily represented as amateurs, the antithesis of serious historical scholarship.[43] Dichotomies such as these – objective versus subjective, professional versus amateur, masculine versus feminine – sustained this shortened historiographical narrative which represents the 1960s as the dawn of a new era which rescued the subject out of the damaging hands of the dilettantes.[44]

The resulting omission of White and Burr is both unjust – Trevor-Roper's essay drew heavily on Burr's scholarship, as Thomas slyly noted – and a form of poetic justice.[45] Indeed, their elision from the historiographical narrative

---

[39] Trevor-Roper, 'The European Witch-Craze', p. 107, n. 45. Emphasis added.

[40] Thomas, *Religion and the Decline of Magic*, p. 436, bibliographical note.

[41] Thomas, *Religion and the Decline of Magic*, p. 516n; Murray, *My First Hundred Years*. On the reception of Murray's work, see also Simpson, 'Margaret Murray'. Norman Cohn held the recent 'extraordinary proliferation of "witches' covens"' against Murray: Cohn, *Europe's Inner Demons*, p. 108.

[42] On Murray's working methods, see Oates, *A Coven of Scholars*. For a discussion of criticism of Murray, see Purkiss, *The Witch in History*, p. 63.

[43] Although employed by University College London, Murray was in fact based in the Egyptology department. Even in that career, she was largely an auto-didact (and proud of it): Murray, *My First Hundred Years*, pp. 93–6. In his refutation of Murray, Norman Cohn not only drew attention to her status as an amateur – she 'was not by profession a historian' – but also to her age – she 'was nearly sixty': Cohn, *Europe's Inner Demons*, p. 109.

[44] See, for instance, Malcolm Gaskill's representation of Trevor-Roper's essay as 'a watershed in modern scholarship [which] banished the earlier twentieth-century idea that real witches had been targeted': Gaskill, 'The Pursuit of Reality', p. 33.

[45] Thomas notes that Trevor-Roper made 'spirited use' of material introduced and partly edited by Burr: Thomas, *Religion and the Decline of Magic*, p. 435, bibliographical note. Trevor-Roper's enmity towards Thomas was notorious. To a correspondent he admitted he was rash to tackle

accidentally stemmed from the same gendered oppositions that we shall find embedded in their writings. These attitudes were part of the way the two men saw themselves as warriors committed to making witchcraft history. A study of White and Burr's scholarship therefore is also important for three historiographical reasons. First of all, it makes the perhaps mundane but hopefully valuable point that early witchcraft historiography was much more diverse than the focus on the 'eccentrics' allows. Secondly, and consequently, it reveals the extent to which witchcraft historiography, a field typically regarded as shaped more by feminist scholarship, has been forged by scholarly masculinity. As Trevor-Roper's comments about Murray show, White and Burr were not the last historians to fashion their identities out of their own opposition to (feminine) 'unreason'.[46] Finally, while White and particularly Burr's scholarship in their explicit rejection of the 'realism' of witchcraft may feel more 'modern' than Murray's or Summers's, their scholarly personae also produced real blind spots.[47] White and Burr produced an apocalyptic vision of the witch-hunt, of good versus evil, in which the accused themselves – and, by extension, women – barely featured. They banished witchcraft to the past as a way of legitimating their own battles in the present.

In addition to their contribution to popular perceptions of witchcraft, then, White and Burr's work on the early modern witch-hunt has had long-lasting historiographical consequences that later generations have struggled to recognize and overcome. While all history may be contemporary history, the pre-occupations and practices of past historians have ways of shaping the views of their successors in ways they do not recognize. The impact of White and Burr's scholarship was not pre-determined, nor did these effects play themselves out solely in gendered terms. For instance, the progress narratives also intersected with White and Burr's high regard for recently unified Germany and its modern research universities which ultimately cast a long shadow on later witchcraft historiography that they could not possibly have foreseen. This study will show that there is real value in taking stock and examining the longer history of our own field. Stripped of its narrative of steady progress, the study of *longue durée* witchcraft historiography can even inform current research questions.

---

a topic as vast as the witch-hunt, 'but it will annoy Keith Thomas, which (I suppose) is something': Sisman, *Hugh Trevor-Roper*, p. 378. Trevor-Roper may also have prevented Thomas from succeeding him as Regius Professor of History at Oxford: ibid., p. 452.

[46] See Purkiss, *The Witch in History*, chap. 3, and, in particular, her especially insightful discussion of historians identifying with male sceptics, pp. 63–5. Trevor-Roper also published an essay on Erasmus and had a portrait of the humanist on his wall: Sisman, *Hugh Trevor-Roper*, pp. 261–2.

[47] For the concept of the 'scholarly persona', see Daston and Sibum, 'Introduction'; and as applied to the historian: Paul, 'What Is a Scholarly Persona?'

Finally, there are more meditative reasons why a study of Andrew Dickson White and George Lincoln Burr and their engagement with witchcraft history may be of interest to historians, regardless of their time period, speciality, or general interest. Their striking use of the past as a place of banishment – a storeroom where those aspects of humanity of which they disapproved could gather dust – brings out the tensions between objectivity and subjectivity in historical writing, between the writing of history and the reasons for history writing. Where historiography often underscores how historians were products of their own time, what follows explores the deeply personal interactions out of which their research emerged. For this reason, we shall begin our case study *in media res*, at the point when our two historians encounter a new heroic witchcraft sceptic but start to have their doubts about the *bona fides* of another. These discoveries also begin to reshape the dynamic between White and Burr, ultimately leading the student to develop a different rationale for the war on witchcraft from his teacher.

From a distance of a century and a half, we can observe quite clearly how the two men's scholarship was constructed out of their relationships with each other, as teacher and student, and with their principal research subjects, the witchcraft sceptics. As we shall see, these relationships and attitudes were not static and they changed over time. Burr's view of human progress differed from White's in subtle yet important ways, and careful reading of their correspondence and his writings shows how the younger scholar struggled to emancipate himself from the person who – quite literally – had lifted him up from the back of the classroom.[48] These relational aspects of their scholarship may also foster introspection – or at least they did for me. Writing this study raised a series of deeply personal questions: how have my teachers shaped my thinking, and what debts do I owe them?[49] How do I relate to my subjects of study? How does my deployment of empathy inflect my scholarship? While there will be as many answers as there are readers to these questions, the case study that follows may also be a useful vehicle for such personal reflection.

2 Two Historians on a Double Date: White and Burr Meet Flade and Loos

There is no better place to begin a study of Andrew Dickson White and George Lincoln Burr then with the letter which showed the first fractures in their relationship. On 10 September 1885, the 28-year old Burr wrote from Trier,

---

[48] White, *Autobiography*, vol. I, pp. 382–3.
[49] I am writing this as a question asking historians about their 'intellectual grandparents' is doing the rounds again on Twitter.

Germany, to White, his erstwhile teacher at Cornell University and its first president, with an unsettling revelation – the person he had been studying for his doctoral dissertation might not be deserving of his time.[50] The young American had been in Europe at White's expense for more than a year, studying at its universities and scouring its bookshops for early modern books and manuscripts, especially witchcraft ones.[51] At the start of 1885, while studying at Leipzig, Burr had settled on a subject for his doctoral dissertation: an edition of a manuscript that was already in White's possession. 'What do you think', he asked White in January, 'of my editing the Flade MS – with perhaps a historical introduction on the growth of the witchcraft superstition [and] the struggle to eradicate it – as a thesis for my doctorate?'[52] Dietrich Flade – a leading judge in Trier, one-time rector of its university, and councillor to its Prince-Elector – had been executed for the crime of witchcraft on 18 September 1589. He was the early modern witch-hunt's 'most eminent victim in the land of its greatest thoroughness': Germany.[53] The judge was reputed to have been an opponent of the hunt. When the Jesuit demonologist Martin Delrio (1551–1608) argued that they 'who defend witches out of their own free will and attempt to lessen the enormity of their crime' should be suspected of witchcraft, he cited Flade as an example who 'was consumed by deadly fires'.[54]

During the spring and summer of 1885 Burr continued to work, on and off, on his Flade project, after White arranged for the manuscript in his collection to be sent to him.[55] In July Burr wrote that he had found further evidence to sustain the judge's heroic reputation. Burr had unearthed an unspecified 'little matter regarding [Flade] which has escaped the notice of his biographers – and all to his credit. It will be a pleasure to show it to you'.[56] Yet, by September 1885, the doubts as to Flade's heroism had evidently set in. To White, who was then presiding over the second meeting of the American Historical Association at

---

[50] Burr to White. Trier, 10 September 1885.

[51] See Burr to White. 'Off Land's End', 19 July 1884, in which Burr announced his arrival in Plymouth the next day. Burr's time in Germany receives a passing mention in Werner, *The Transatlantic World of Higher Education*, esp. pp. 84, 184, 246.

[52] Burr to White. Leipzig, 7 January 1885.

[53] Burr, 'The Fate of Dietrich Flade', p. 190. Voltmer, 'Witch-Finders, Witch-Hunters or Kings of the Sabbath?', pp. 82–3, has shown that Flade had, in fact, sentenced eight women to death for the crime of witchcraft.

[54] Delrio, *Disquisitionum magicarum libri sex*, vol. III, 28: 'quis patrocinatur sponte maleficis, et conatur criminis enormitatem elevare, et contendit, non esse credendum iis, quae de illis certo narrantur, et ea omnia vana esse et delira, aliaque huiusmodi . . . flammis feralibus consumptus fuit'.

[55] White to Burr. Ithaca, NY, 14 February 1885; Burr to White. Salzburg, 19 March 1885. Burr arranged a shipment of books for White but kept three as possibly of use 'in my work on the Flade matter'.

[56] Burr to White. Zurich, July 21, 1885.

Saratoga Springs, New York, Burr confessed his scepticism as to whether the judge really deserved his reputation as a martyr: 'I am much puzzled as to whether it is worth the while to give to the world what may only deprive the unfortunate man of the scanty recognition which he has thus far received'.[57]

Fortunately for Burr, the setback was only temporary. While Flade may not have been a true sceptic, he could still have fallen victim to a great Jesuit conspiracy. His discovery of their *litterae annuae* (the annual reports written by Jesuit colleges) led Burr to excitedly report on a secret Jesuit plot – 'they stand virtually convicted out of their own mouths' – to use a fourteen-year-old boy from the countryside to incriminate Flade: 'Of course, in the MSS fallen into my hands, the story of the boy is told, as if in good faith, but what was credible enough to deceive those for who the report was destined in that day, is quite too transparent in ours'.[58] Moreover, if Burr had been disappointed in Flade, he soon located in the Trier city library a manuscript belonging to another witchcraft sceptic more deserving of praise. On 10 June 1886, Burr sent White 'a very crazy letter' – the discovery of Cornelius Loos's 'long-lost manuscript (the book *De vera et falsa magia* which cost him humiliation, misery and death)' disturbed Burr's 'mental equilibrium'.[59] Where the Flade manuscript had been a disappointment, that of Loos was 'the boldest thing ever written against the witchcraft horror, and the most eloquent except perhaps [Friedrich] Spee's *Cautio [criminalis]*'.[60] Martin Delrio had excoriated Loos – 'may God have mercy on his soul' – on the same page of his demonology as he denounced Flade, and he included the priest's forced abjuration as an appendix to his witchcraft tome.[61] In October 1886, a month after his return from Europe to Cornell University, Burr gave a lecture on Flade, who 'had met his death', and Loos, 'one of [the world's] bravest souls', in which he speculated about the horrors used to force the latter's recantation.[62] Burr's manuscript discovery was even announced to the American public by Charles Kendall Adams, White's successor as University President, on 11 November 1886, in an article for *The Nation* newspaper entitled 'A Manuscript and a Man'.[63]

---

[57] Burr to White. Trier, 10 September 1885.

[58] Burr to White. Trier, April 18, 1886. Jesuit *litterae annuae* provide a rich source of information on the early modern witch-hunt, especially in Germany: Sobiech, *Jesuit Prison Ministry in the Witch Trials of the Holy Roman Empire.*

[59] Burr to White. Trier, 10 June 1886. The historiography on Loos has been dominated by amateur historians who praise him as 'ein kritischer Geist' and attack his opponents: P. C. Van der Eerden, 'Der Teufelspakt bei Binsfeld und Loos', p. 72; or they provide Loos with an epitaph: Othon Scholer, '"O Kehricht des Aberglaubens"', p. 270.

[60] Burr to White. Trier, 14 June 1886.

[61] Delrio, *Disquisitionum magicarum libri sex*, vol. III, p. 28: 'cuius animae Deus parcat'; ibid., vol. III, pp. 117–19.

[62] Burr, 'On the Loos Manuscript', pp. 151, 153.   [63] Adams, 'A Manuscript and a Man'.

Burr's work on the trial of Dr Flade and his discovery of the Loos manuscript, as part as his doctoral dissertation, mark the arrival of witchcraft history within the halls of academia, which were beginning to welcome history as a discipline around this time.[64] While Burr's contributions to this new field are scarcely remembered today for reasons already discussed, his interests were also not fully his own. Burr was, to a considerable degree, Andrew Dickson White's creation. Burr's work on the history of witchcraft was part of White's much bigger project on the history of science, which, in turn, was also a project of moral and religious reform. Burr's letter of 10 September 1885 casting doubt on Flade's heroism marked the first sign of dissension within the ranks.

Burr first met Andrew Dickson White, Cornell University's co-founder, first president, and first professor of history, in the autumn of 1878, when as a mere sophomore he attended White's senior class on the historical development of criminal law, in which the witch-hunt played a major role.[65] In terms of social status the two men could hardly have been more different. White, who was Burr's senior by twenty-four years, was the heir to a considerable fortune. Education and public service were for him a vocation and a duty rather than a form of employment.[66] Burr, by contrast, had worked as a schoolteacher and apprentice printer to save money for college.[67] Yet White's teaching left Burr enthralled. Fifty years later he still recalled White bringing his personal copy of the *Malleus maleficarum* to class, 'which he told us had caused more suffering than any other product of the human pen'.[68] Burr, at the same time, also made an impact on White, who was so impressed by the quality of Burr's essays he asked the sophomore to mark the work of his classmates – in secret, 'for had the seniors known that I had intrusted their papers to the tender mercies of a sophomore, they would probably have mobbed me'.[69] After that first appointment as examiner, Burr would remain in

---

[64] On the professionalisation of history, see Lingelbach, 'The Institutionalization and Professionalization of History'. I am separating the *historical* study of witchcraft from earlier discussions of witchcraft and its possible reality. The law and theology faculties of early modern universities were often consulted on witchcraft matters, and aspects of demonology were the subject of early modern academic disputations. See, e.g., Kauertz, *Wissenschaft und Hexenglaube*; Meyer, 'Systematische Theologie, katechetische Strenge und pädagogisches Augenmaß'.

[65] In his journal entry for Wednesday 8 November 1878, White noted that he was 'at work on final part of lecture on Demoniacal Powers which I delivered at noon': Ogden (ed.), *The Diaries of Andrew D. White*, p. 199. Giving his thoughts on publishing White's lectures, Burr discussed 'the lectures on witchcraft, demoniacal possession, and torture': Burr to White. Zurich, 7 July 1885.

[66] Horace White, a wealthy banker and railroad man, left his son a sizable fortune on his death in 1860: Altschuler, *Andrew D. White*, pp. 22, 42.

[67] Bainton, 'His Life', pp. 11–14.

[68] Burr, 'A Witch-Hunter in the Book-Shops', p. 294. On Burr's first encounter with White and witchcraft, see also the footnote, written in April 1938, two months before Burr's death on 27 June: Burr, 'Introduction to Lea's Materials toward a History of Witchcraft', p. 455.

[69] White, *Autobiography of Andrew Dickson White*, vol. I, pp. 382–3.

the employment of White and, later, Cornell University until his retirement. During White's vacations and diplomatic assignments in Europe, Burr even moved into the White family home on campus.[70] In 1907 Burr, then aged fifty, married a former student, but the marriage ended tragically with the death of both mother and infant in childbirth less than two years later.[71] Burr, then, remained principally known as White's disciple. At his retirement in 1922 the local newspaper described him as 'for many years a member of [White's] household ... and now his literary executor, having remained his intimate friend until death'.[72]

This Element argues for the important role that relational identities and scholarly personae played (and doubtless still play) in the production of historical scholarship. While this is an aspect of historiography that is often overlooked, it has certainly not been the approach which historians of science have taken towards White (Figure 2). (Burr, as already noted, has been almost entirely overlooked.) When they are not refuting him, historians of science have treated White simply as a man of his times, which of course he in many ways was. One admiring reviewer of Charles Darwin's 1859 *On the Origin of Species*, for instance, wrote that 'extinguished theologians lie about the cradle of every science as the strangled snakes beside that of Hercules' – language that could easily have been uttered by White.[73] Although the *Warfare of Science* was considered the more erudite and influential work, it was (and is) also commonly placed alongside John William Draper's *History of the Conflict between Religion and Science* (1874).[74] (The supposed conflict between science and religion has also been called the Draper-White thesis.[75]) Many of White's ideas were firmly rooted in late nineteenth-century America. His belief in progress was almost axiomatic – in his obituary of White, Burr would draw special attention to it – but it was also an important influence on his contemporaries.[76] White's promotion of evolutionary processes within human society (as opposed revolutionary ones) reflected both the times in which he lived and his elite social standing.[77] His argument that Christianity effectively required another Reformation – as its full title made clear, *Warfare* was aimed at 'theology', *not* religion – was shared by many liberal Protestants, while others used his arguments to go further still.[78] His belief in the inhibitory role of religious dogma was similarly widespread,

---

[70] University of Pennsylvania, MS Coll. 111: Henry Charles Lea papers, Box 4, Folder 208. Ithaca, NY, 11 January 1895.

[71] Bainton, 'His Life', pp. 96–107.   [72] 'Retires in February: G. L. Burr'.

[73] Dixon, *Science and Religion*, p. 2.

[74] Draper, *History of the Conflict between Religion and Science*. On the greater importance of *Warfare of Science*, see Lindberg and Numbers, 'Beyond War and Peace', p. 340.

[75] See e.g. the introduction to Ferngren, *Science and Religion*, p. ix.

[76] Burr, 'Andrew Dickson White', p. 416. See also Altschuler, *Andrew D. White*, p. 16.

[77] Hawkins, *Social Darwinism in European and American Thought*.

[78] Ungureanu, 'Science and Religion in the Anglo-American Periodical Press'.

Figure 2 Andrew Dickson White (1885). Image courtesy of Cornell University Library.

leading Peter Harrison to conclude that 'all that remained [for White and for Draper] was to fill in the blanks'.[79] As a result, White's biography hardly features. At most, White is represented as defending the reputation of Cornell University, the institution he had helped to found as the country's first non-sectarian (and therefore in the eyes of its opponents, 'godless') university.[80]

While these are extremely valuable insights, treating White solely as a product of his time elides a substantial part of the *Warfare of Science*'s origins and significance, its author's persona, and the wider project to which the book – like Burr's witchcraft writings – was meant to contribute. White and Burr found themselves outside the mainstream on several fronts, most notably within history as a newly emerging professional discipline. While *Warfare* was one of the earliest works of history of science, it was self-consciously not a work of *scientific* history. Although White was a cheerleader for all things German (its

---

[79] Harrison, 'That Religion Has Typically Impeded the Progress of Science', p. 200.
[80] Numbers (ed.), introduction to *Galileo Goes to Jail*, pp. 2–3; Brooke, *Science and Religion*, pp. 46–7. For the label 'godless', see White, *Autobiography*, vol. I, p. 125.

universities and historical research included),[81] in practice his mode of scholarship was aligned more with that of the early nineteenth-century 'gentleman amateur' and the traditional belief in *historia magistra vitae* than with the new ideal of scientific objectivity.[82] (Burr, as we shall see, would echo White's beliefs.) Similarly, White's religious vision of Christianity stripped off all dogma was genuinely esoteric – he himself struggled to define it – and moved well beyond liberal Protestantism. White's biographer Glenn C. Altschuler identified his subject's 'vagueness' about doctrine as 'a product of confusion and, perhaps unconsciously, of a refusal to accept the unsettling implications of his own thought'.[83] A more plausible, if paradoxical, reading is that faith for White was a genuinely mystical experience, beyond words or description. As this suggests, White saw and presented himself as a religious reformer, the latest in a long line of *devout* great men – both scientists and witchcraft sceptics – whose defender he was. White's identity as a reformer sustained a project that extended beyond history, religion, or science. *Warfare* was part of a larger project of reforming both knowledge and mankind, which White not only committed to paper but also sought to put into practice at Cornell.[84] This project cannot be understood without analysis of White's identity as a reformer and his relationship with Burr, without whose assistance *Warfare* would never have appeared.

A close reading of White and Burr's letters and publications, then, complicates many of the grand narratives that the main historiographical models have used as a shorthand for nineteenth-century scholarship: not only the 'conflict' thesis in history of science, but also the very similar 'rationalist' paradigm in witchcraft history, and, lying beyond that, Rankean 'realism' – the nineteenth-century pursuit of writing history 'objectively', as it 'actually' was. They present a vital case study of the role of scholarly personae and relational identities in the production of historical knowledge. Their scholarship was in

---

[81] White, 'On Studies in General History and the History of Civilization', pp. 69–70. See also White, 'The New Germany', p. 242.

[82] Novick, *That Noble Dream*, esp. chap. 2; Iggers, 'The Intellectual Foundations of Nineteenth-Century "Scientific" History'. White, 'On Studies in General History', pp. 49, 53, 60, repeatedly praised such traditional 'gentleman amateurs' as John Lothrop Motley and William H. Prescott. In her short pamphlet on White's tenure at the University of Michigan, Ruth Bordin observed that White 'was soon supplanted by other young men' who 'developed a professionalization of the discipline with which White was only partly in sympathy': Bordin, *Andrew Dickson White*, p. 17.

[83] Altschuler, *Andrew D. White*, p. 212.

[84] See, for instance, his comment that 'training men to think, speak, and write on such subjects in the light of the best modern thought and experience [will bring] the results obtained by University research to bear upon the people at large': White, *Evolution and Revolution*, p. 17. My choice here of 'mankind' over humanity or humankind is intentional and meant to reflect White's gendered attitudes, not my own.

important ways a relational construct, shaped – dictated, even – by the bond between White and Burr, and *with* their historical subjects, Cornelius Loos and Dietrich Flade foremost among them. These ties meant that, despite Burr's doubts, Flade remained something of a martyr for him. Moreover, if these homosocial relationships, with the past and in the present, underpinned their scholarship, they were also the product of a particular vision of manhood. The early modern witch-hunt played a seminal role within this project, in part because it transformed the struggle against 'unreason' into a rescue mission. The battle against the witchcraft 'delusion' offered an avenue for heroic *male* sceptics to rescue damsels in distress, with highly gendered wider implications for how they and other scientific apostles of progress were presented and understood. If the practices of nineteenth-century historical research were fundamentally gendered, as Joan W. Scott, Bonnie G. Smith, Angelika Epple, and others have taught us, this Element analyses these important homosocial relationships to show how gendered the fruits of such scholarship really were.[85] Before we can analyse these relationships further, however, the wider contours of White's reform project and the role of history within it need to be sketched out in more detail, both as the stage on which these scholarly personae and relationships were enacted and as the pursuit which legitimated everything else.

3 History and a Reformer's Project of Reform

White was always explicit about the moral purpose that should underpin history writing. In his 1884 presidential address to the American Historical Association – the organization's first – he stressed that the pursuit of morality was the only proper motive to write history: 'The great, deep ground out of which large historical studies may grow is the ethical ground – the simple ethical necessity for the perfecting, first, of man as man, and, secondly, of man as a member of society.'[86] Indeed, White had denounced knowledge for its own sake from his undergraduate days onwards. In his *Autobiography* he dismissed the teaching he received at Yale College in the early 1850s as 'gerund-grinding'.[87] In his first magazine article he denounced 'chronology-spinners and accent-markers' and those who 'counterfeit' history: 'sham

---

[85] Scott, *Gender and the Politics of History*; Smith, 'Gender and the Practices of Scientific History'; Smith, *The Gender of History*. See also Alberti, *Gender and the Historian*, pp. 1–20; Epple, 'Historiographiegeschichte als Diskursanalyse und Analytik der Macht'; Schnicke, *Die männliche Disziplin*.
[86] White, 'On Studies in General History', p. 51.
[87] White, 'Glimpses of Universal History', pp. 398–9. Although his biographer notes that 'there is no evidence of dissatisfaction at the time', the footnote below suggests that White's criticism of knowledge for its own sake can be dated to an early time of his life: Altschuler, *Andrew D. White*, p. 28.

historians – the real infidels of these times – men who see in this world's great rich history, a mere game at cross-purposes, a careless whirl'.[88] In his undergraduate lecture series 'on History', first at the University of Michigan and later at Cornell, White included similar stark warnings about 'the dealers in Sham History and their utterances'.[89] His youthful historical essays from the early 1860s already attempted to put into practice this deeply held belief that the past held in store moral lessons for the present. During the American Civil War his essays on Thomas Jefferson, on Cardinal Richelieu, and on the history of Russian serfdom repackaged history to advance the abolitionist cause.[90] The French statesman, a Unionist *avant la lettre*, was depicted as having 'taught the true method ... of strangling that worst foe of liberty and order in every age – a serf-owning aristocracy'.[91]

Historical scholarship for White not only served to legitimate future reform, however. It was also a product and a well-connected part of the overarching reform project. The *Warfare of Science*, for instance, was not only a polemical intervention in a public debate, it was also dedicated to the memory of Ezra Cornell and intended as a 'tribute' to the university he and White had co-founded.[92] Perhaps as a result, White's historical scholarship shares essential features with the reforms he championed. First of all, White's commitment to reform was less radical than he pretended, just as his flowing prose often concealed a more conservative stance – a factor complicating the interpretation of his writings.[93] White's causes – the reform of Higher Education and the Civil Service, and even abolitionism – were safe for a man of independent means, because as the son of a wealthy banker from Syracuse, New York, he simply took for granted that meritocracy would legitimate, rather than challenge, the position of white men of his social standing.[94] Secondly, the same causes (especially Higher Education reform) also implied a link between the perfecting of 'man' and society, and indirectly between the Great Man and his (general) cause, that permeated all of White's historical writings. His understanding of

---

[88] White, 'Glimpses of Universal History', pp. 398–9.

[89] White, *Outlines of a Course of Lectures on History* (1861), p. 4; White, *Outlines of a Course of Lectures on History* (1870), p. 8.

[90] White, 'Jefferson and Slavery'; White, 'The Statesmanship of Richelieu'; White, 'The Development and Overthrow of the Russian Serf-System'.

[91] White, 'The Statesmanship of Richelieu', p. 624.

[92] White, *Warfare* (1896), vol. I, pp. iii, xi; White also donated the royalties to the President White Library at Cornell University: Bainton, 'His Life', p. 52.

[93] Here I am extending a central insight of Glen C. Altschuler's biography ('White liked to think of himself as a radical, but in reality his radicalism was severely limited. Most of his fire was rhetorical') to White's historical writings: Altschuler, *Andrew D. White*, p. 19.

[94] E.g. on 'White's elitist assumptions about education': Altschuler, *Andrew D. White*, p. 37.

both the past and the present, then, were sustained by the idea that society can be improved by the moral improvement of individuals.

This preoccupation with general causes, evident for instance in White's 1884 presidential address to the American Historical Association, has led both Georg G. Iggers and Dorothy Ross to observe that White understood Leopold von Ranke's idealistic philosophy of history better than most of his American contemporaries.[95] The supposed founder of modern history writing, who had described nations as 'spiritual substances ... thoughts of God', was understood and valued in the United States almost exclusively as the objective empiricist who studied 'how things actually were'.[96] White once identified his central and frequently stated belief in 'the higher and better development of man ... as a *man*' as German in origin, but this may have been more the result of White's Germanophilia (all good things came from Germany) than his reception of German scholarship.[97] Although the American Historical Association's first president appears to have been an outlier within a profession which increasingly valued 'scientific objectivity', his negative depiction of Ranke (discussed in Section 5 below) suggests that this was not because of a more perfect understanding of Rankean philosophy of history.[98] Germany, perceived as an idea and an ideal, seems to have been much more important to White than its historical methods.

In fact, Germany and its history illustrate White's historical interests perfectly. The German past and present contained both his two great historical interests – science and witchcraft – and revealed, at least to him, how general causes and great individuals intersected in history. In an 1882 public lecture entitled 'The New Germany', White presented German unification in the same moral terms as the abolition of slavery, even going so far as to suggest that it was 'perhaps' more 'striking' as well.[99] He was awed by Germany's 'long-continued sacrifice, and work, and struggle ... not merely by victory over other powers, but, far more, by victory over herself – over tendencies to sloth, anarchy, unreason'.[100] White placed the nadir of Germany's 'political',

---

[95] Iggers, 'The Image of Ranke in American and German Historical Thought', esp. p. 19; Ross, 'On the Misunderstanding of Ranke', esp. p. 165.

[96] Novick, *That Noble Dream*, chap. 1, esp. p. 27.

[97] White, *Some Practical Influences of German Thought*, p. 12. Italics in original.

[98] White's presidential address can best be read as an attempt to find a home for 'general' or 'philosophical' history (which offered practitioners 'a means for the greater enlightenment of their country and the better development of mankind') within an Association apparently devoted to 'special' history, examples of which are criticized for dealing merely with 'surface facts': White, 'On Studies in General History', pp. 72, 55.

[99] White, 'The New Germany', p. 205. According to his diary, White delivered this 'very well rec'd' lecture in New York on 20 December 1882: Ogden (ed.), *The Diaries of Andrew D. White*, p. 230.

[100] White, 'The New Germany', p. 206.

'intellectual', and 'moral development' in the seventeenth century. The 'golden age of witchcraft persecution' was, for White, 'the golden age of bigots and pedants'.[101] Witchcraft illustrated an earlier, opposite state of affairs, while its pastness emphasized how far Germany had come. The early modern period saw university 'instructors bec[o]me more and more stupid and the students more and more imbruted' – the contrast with the present, where German research universities provided a model for the world, could not be starker.[102] The period of the Thirty Years War allowed White to show 'the evolution of a higher activity out of a lower by patient thought and earnest effort', and how generations of 'strong men' had 'persevered in this effort to evolve Cosmos out of Chaos'.[103] To some extent, these men fought to transcend general causes, notably Germany's geography, surrounded as it was by hostile nations.[104] Yet they principally succeeded by aligning themselves *with* general causes and against those who resisted them, anticipating the recurring conflict between reactionaries and 'the thinking, open-minded, devoted men ... who are evidently thinking the future thought of the world' which sustained the *Warfare of Science*.[105] White, accordingly, ended his lecture with an extended tribute to the architect of German unification, Prince Otto von Bismarck, whom he had met as US minister to Germany.[106]

Aligning great men and general causes – also construed as 'laws of development' and even as 'Providence' – made their success, and thus their progress, inevitable.[107] This was to some extent a double-edged sword, however. If the general causes were forces for good (which they almost always were), then their inevitability possessed evident appeal. Yet the same inevitability could also undercut the practical call to action. Making men such as Bismarck into history's principal agents of change enabled White to infuse a measure of human agency into this inevitable march of progress. The role of the historian in retrospectively discerning general causes might defuse the tension between inevitability and agency even more. White's undergraduate lecture on Erasmus

---

[101] White, 'The New Germany', p. 214.

[102] White, 'The New Germany', pp. 213–14. On the German origins of the modern research university, see Clark, *Academic Charisma*.

[103] White, 'The New Germany', p. 225. This attitude towards German progress constitutes a little noticed but important part of the *Warfare of Science* as well. See e.g. White's discussion of comets: White, *Warfare* (1896), vol. I, pp. 182, 201.

[104] White, 'The New Germany', p. 207. [105] White, *Warfare* (1896), vol. I, p. 319.

[106] White had been US minister to Germany from 1879 to 1881 and would return as ambassador from 1897 to 1902: Altschuler, *Andrew D. White*, pp. 119–31, 234–47. Bismarck's would be the last (and longest) of the seven portraits included in Andrew Dickson White, *Seven Great Statesmen*, pp. 391–535.

[107] For 'laws of development', see White, 'On Studies in General History', p. 51; for an example of 'Providence', see White, *Autobiography*, vol. I, p. 75.

thus counselled that philosophical history which 'reverently' approached the 'secret hand of God' should be combined with biography – that is, 'the close study of the life [and] work of the <u>great men</u> who were the direct agents in the [historical] work'.[108]

While discerning the hand of God might appear almost a mystical experience, in practice White's attention mostly centred on the agents supposedly doing His work. Most of his undergraduate lectures, as the first history of Cornell University noted, focussed on 'individual men as representative of movements', 'elaborate studies of the lives of great artists', 'the influence of the founders of the great religious orders', and 'studies in abnormal opinions' – that is, those scholastics who dared to oppose science.[109] The same preoccupation with great men can be discerned from the title of White's second, lesser-known monograph: *Seven Great Statesmen in the Warfare of Humanity with Unreason* (1910), which – much like *Warfare of Science* – was based on his lectures and which was originally meant to chart the founding of modern Germany. ('The Builders of Modern Germany' was one possible title White had mentioned in discussions with Burr.[110]) Its portrayal of Hugo Grotius (whom White considered an honorary German) shows both the extent of White's hero worship and the religious language of his writings. Grotius was another Saviour, born for the 'redemption of civilization', who after his death, as 'a martyr to unreason', had 'risen from the dead, and live[s] evermore' [cf. Revelation 1:18] within a whole host of modern institutions and 'in the heart and mind of every man who worthily undertakes to serve the nobler purposes of his country or the larger interests of his race'.[111]

The same principles – notably the role of individuals as agents of change – and religious language shaped White's famous lecture at Cooper Union in New York City on 17 December 1869, on 'the Battle-Fields of Science', the first public outing of what would become the *Warfare of Science*.[112] Study of this lecture allows us to flesh out the strong religious impetus behind White's project, and how he conceived of his own role within it. Both factors were considerably stronger motives than White's commonly cited desire to defend

---

[108] Andrew Dickson White, 'Erasmus', pp. 2–3 (Ithaca, NY, Cornell University Rare and Manuscript Collections, Andrew Dickson White Microfilm Collection, reel 140, p. 144). Underlining in the original manuscript.

[109] Hewett, *Cornell University*, vol. I, pp. 181–2. Bordin similarly observed that Michigan White's 'approach to the teaching of history was largely biographical': Bordin, *Andrew Dickson White*, p. 15.

[110] White to Burr. Ithaca, NY, 20 June 1896.

[111] White, *Seven Great Statesmen*, pp. 55, 101. As president of the American delegation to the 1899 Hague Peace Conference, White laid a wreath on Grotius's tomb and gave a speech wrapped in similar religious language: *Proceedings at the Laying of a Wreath*.

[112] White, 'The Battle-Fields of Science'.

Cornell University from sectarian attacks.[113] In his lecture White maintained that 'all untrammeled scientific investigation ... has invariably resulted in the highest good of Religion and Science'.[114] Christianity has 'given hope to the hopeless, comfort to the afflicted, light to the blind, bread to the starving, [and] life to the dying'; only 'the idea that purely scientific investigation is unsafe' had sent it off kilter.[115] From the outset, then, White's project was as much one of religious reform as a vindication of science, his strident tone notwithstanding. Unlike Draper, White believed the problem was with 'dogmatic theology', with 'the dead husks of sect and dogma', not with religion itself.[116] Here, too, God revealed the proper pursuit of science through history, rather than theology: 'The very finger of the Almighty has written on history that science must be studied by means proper to itself, and in no other way.' Inevitably, White substantiated these claims by populating the battle-fields with devout Christian scientists: Copernicus 'had lived a pious, Christian life', while Kepler 'speaks as one inspired'. Others were martyrs, whether proverbial or real: Galileo 'was subject certainly to indignity and imprisonment – possibly to physical torture'; Vesalius died 'on a pilgrimage to the Holy Land to atone for his sin [i.e. his anatomical discoveries] ... His poor blind foes destroyed one of *religion's* greatest apostles.'[117]

Witchcraft accusations were woven into the *Warfare of Science* project from the outset. Not only were supposed opponents of the witch-hunt such as Dietrich Flade burnt as witches, scientists were transformed into sorcerers as well. In his 1869 lecture White reported that the thirteenth-century physician Arnold de Villanova 'was charged with sorcery and dealings with the devil'.[118] In his undergraduate lecture on the Age of Discovery, he declared that the compass was well known among medieval mariners, 'yet to no small extent, dread of the charge of sorcery prevented its use'.[119] Similarly, the lecture on 'The Invention of Printing' asserted that England's first printer, William Caxton, 'did not escape the charge of sorcery'.[120] In 1876, when the *Warfare of Science* had grown from a published lecture to a small book, White claimed that 'mediaeval

---

[113] Lindberg and Numbers, 'Beyond War and Peace', p. 338; Brooke, *Science and Religion*, 46–7.
[114] White, 'The Battle-Fields of Science'.
[115] White, 'The Battle-Fields of Science'. Note the imitation of the Beatitudes.
[116] For White's thoughts on Draper's *History of the Conflict between Religion and Science*, see White, *Warfare* (1896), vol. I, p. ix. For White's comment about 'husks', see White, *Warfare* (1876), p. 151. I disagree, therefore, with claims that White narrowed his attack on religion only with time: Lindberg and Numbers, 'Beyond War and Peace', p. 339; Russell, *Inventing the Flat Earth*, p. 42.
[117] White, 'The Battle-Fields of Science'. Emphasis added.
[118] White, 'The Battle-Fields of Science'.
[119] 'The Age of Discovery', p. 8 (WMC, Reel 140, p. 13).
[120] 'The New Diffusion of Thought: B. The Invention of Printing', p. 15 (Reel 140, p. 15)

scientific battle-fields [were] strewed with . . . charge[s] of sorcery, of unlawful compact with the devil', and traced the use of 'these missiles' in almost all fields, and up to the eighteenth century.[121] By 1896 lengthy discussions of witchcraft and demonic possession were inserted into a number of chapters, effectively making the war on witchcraft and the warfare of science extensions of each other.[122] Like the *Warfare of Science*, the witch-hunt demonstrated the consequences of dangerous theological and sectarian ideas, and it enhanced the humanitarian nature of the struggle against unreason in ways those battling purely on the frontlines of science never could: unlike scientists, witchcraft sceptics could be depicted as risking their lives to rescue others.

The 1869 lecture also shows how White joined the war himself. First of all, the historian entered the battlefield alongside the warriors: 'we will look well at the combatants – we will listen to the battle-cries, we will note the strategy of leaders, the cut and thrust of champions, the weight of missiles, the temper of weapons'.[123] Engaged on the same terrain, the historian was not at all different from the subjects he studied as he faced very similar enemies in his own day. When the final two-volume iteration of *Warfare* appeared, Burr, in a biographical sketch, would depict White's religious-scientific mission as similar to those of his subjects: 'he seeks only to lift the timid faith which dares not trust the God of the universe to deal truly with the human mind he has made'.[124] Indeed, White was a combatant in his own right. While witchcraft might be past, the struggle for science was still ongoing. In concluding his 1869 lecture, White referred to 'another battle-field in our own land and time': the attacks against Cornell University, 'against a body of Christian Trustees and Professors earnestly devoted to building up Christian civilization', and against the institution's *other* founder, Ezra Cornell, 'whose life has been one of the purest and noblest on American records'. Both his self-evident role in Cornell's founding and his clarion call that 'the Warfare of Science . . . be changed' to one where 'religion and science shall stand together as allies' allowed White to style himself as the latest (if not the last) in a long line of virtuous Christian men fighting for scientific *and* religious Truth. As such, White cast himself as the embodiment of the values and virtues that he himself had discerned in history in the first place. White's own perceived place in

---

[121] White, *Warfare* (1876), pp. 65, 77, 102, 108. White had also uncovered the witchcraft accusations against Kepler's mother, on which see Rublack, *The Astronomer and the Witch*.

[122] See especially the chapters entitled 'From "Signs and Wonders" to Law in the Heavens', 'From "The Prince of the Power of the Air" to Meteorology', 'From Magic to Chemistry and Physics', 'From Miracles to Medicine', 'From "Demoniacal Possession" to Insanity', and 'From Diabolism to Hysteria'. For charges against reputed 'sorcerers', see White, *Warfare* (1896), vol. I, pp. 107, 111, 319, 354, 377, 386, 390; vol. II, pp. 35, 37, 38.

[123] White, 'The Battle-Fields of Science'.

[124] Burr, 'Sketch of Andrew Dickson White', p. 556.

history, as the heir and successor of generations of other heroic men, profoundly shaped his writings and his actions.

If the importance White attached to his public persona as a reformer is evident from any reading of his works, it is brought into even starker relief by his evident failure to live up to those standards. A recurring problem during White's tenure at Cornell was the willingness of others to take White's rhetoric – for instance, about the University's non-denominational status and its admission policy – to its logical conclusion. White's dismissal of Cornell's first Jewish academic and his role in 'enclosing' its female undergraduates, discussed by White's biographer, offer perfect illustrations of the contrast between White's words and deeds.[125] Yet the possible admission of black students provides an even more instructive example. In a private letter, White declared that he would admit any suitable black candidate 'even if all our five hundred white students were to ask for dismissal on that account'. None, however, were accepted during his twenty-year tenure, and White made no discernible effort to advertise his views publicly. He did, however, preserve a copy of his claim for his personal records.[126] White's rhetorical fireworks, then, suggest that his reputation as a radical reformer mattered rather more than the practical implementation of reform. That insight should also shape our interpretation of White's historical writings as works more radical in appearance than in fact – and more committed to narrative than to facts.

4 The Reformer's Apprentice

If the *Warfare of Science* was a project of religious reform – one that transformed early scientists into religious reformers (and suspected sorcerers) and replaced theology with history – then White would find in Burr a willing collaborator. Not only because 'the *Warfare of Science* was a crusade, and Burr loved a crusade', as Roland Bainton, Burr's friend and biographer, later put it, but also because Burr was himself as deeply religious and as religiously heterodox as his patron.[127] Burr told White that, 'had my personal creed been more orthodox and had I been able to see in religion a panacea for all the ills of the earth', he might have become a minister, but he chose to become a teacher of history instead.[128] In 1891 Burr preached before Cornell's Christian Union on 'the Living Gospel', a text 'written

---

[125] Altschuler, *Andrew D. White*, pp. 68, 97–9, 104–5. See also Altschuler's summary on p. 19: 'Most of [White's] fire was rhetorical. Beneath that rhetoric was the bedrock conservatism common to men of wealth.'

[126] Andrew Dickson White to C. H. McCormick. Ithaca, NY, 5 September 1870. For further details, see: https://diversity.cornell.edu/our-story/our-historic-commitment.

[127] Bainton, 'His Life', p. 49.   [128] Burr to White. Zurich, 13 August 1885.

not on tables of stone or leaves of parchment, but on human lives'.[129] The gospels of
the New Testament were 'but the student-notes of [Christ's] pupils: shall we
measure his teaching by them?'[130] Instead Burr used his sermon to chart 'a single
paragraph from the genealogy of Christian charity'.[131] White similarly had not
confined his praise to scientists alone. Alongside them, he lined up a select group of
good Christian figures, such as (rather implausibly) Carlo Borromeo and Vincent de
Paul, 'who have preached and practised the righteousness of the prophets, and the
aspirations of the Psalmist, and the blessed Sermon on the Mount'.[132] Both men
thus focussed attention away from dogma and onto the (idealized, charitable)
actions of great individuals, in effect replacing theology with history. Burr's
conception of history was accordingly as transcendent as White's – history was
'not a stupid mechanical sequence, but a living principle, inspiring men' – and just
as ethically charged – 'history is not a physical, but a moral science: … not
physiology, but ethics'.[133] Teacher and student had much ground in common, but,
as we shall see, differences in outlook appeared as their relationship developed.

Burr was introduced to his teacher's projects soon after they met at the end of
one of White's classes in the autumn of 1878. The following summer, before the
president departed for Europe, he recommended three books to Burr, two of which
we have already encountered: Lecky's *History of the Rise and Influence of the
Spirit of Rationalism* and Draper's *History of the Conflict between Religion and
Science*.[134] Yet Burr's involvement in White's many writing projects seems to have
begun in earnest only during his stay in Europe in the mid-1880s; as White's
literary executor it would continue until Burr's own death. Travelling through
Europe at his teacher's expense as his 'witch-hunter in the book-shops', Burr was
extremely conscious of the debts he owed his patron. The asymmetrical nature of
their relationship, so unequal in age, wealth, and social status, is encapsulated in the
appellations with which the two men opened their letters. While Burr in White's
letters was sometimes a 'dear friend', and once even a 'busy B.', White for Burr
would remain 'Mr President' long after he had resigned as president of Cornell
University.[135]

---

[129] Burr, 'The Living Gospel', p. 237.   [130] Burr, 'The Living Gospel', p. 241.
[131] Burr, 'The Living Gospel', p. 239.   [132] White, *Warfare* (1876), p. 150.
[133] Burr to White. Zurich, July 10, 1885. Earlier Burr had told White that no lecture series in Europe
    was better than White's, given by 'a man who has not only a brain, but a heart and a conscience':
    Burr to White. Leizpig, 8 December 1884.
[134] Burr to White. Syracuse, NY, 18 July 1879. Burr reported that he had already read Lecky twice.
    The third book was by Henry Thomas Buckle; presumably his *History of Civilization in
    England* (1857), which White praised in his presidential address: White, 'On Studies in
    General History', p. 50.
[135] White to Burr. Ithaca, NY, 3 December 1884: 'My dear Busy B.'; White to Burr. Saratoga
    Springs, NY, 26 August 1885: 'My dear friend'; Burr, 'Andrew Dickson White', p. 415: 'Yet it
    is as "President White" that we shall remember him.'

From the beginning of his European trip, Burr sought to impress White with both his work ethic and with his discoveries. He ostentatiously enjoyed early morning lectures – 'Some American students would be horrified to having a lecture at 7 but it is a feature I decidedly enjoy' – and he worked his way through 'a pile of MSS about six feet high'.[136] He also reported discovering a live bookworm in Trier's copy of the *Malleus maleficarum* – 'horrible fodder, even for such a literary glutton'.[137] The efforts to impress (and perhaps entertain) his patron were part of an attempt to make White's project into a shared endeavour, while still acknowledging that White did not need him. In a letter written on 12 February 1885, Burr told White that he believed that 'I can serve the world best by serving you', at least until White was 'through' with him. Burr confessed that he was also 'by no means certain that I am so well fitted as another to aid you'. Yet he also worked to bridge the physical and emotional distance that separated them. Already on 24 November 1884, the 28-year old used White's poor health to issue a (non-)invitation to join him in Europe: 'if I dared, I would prescribe you a winter trip to Germany'.[138] In February he again urged White to lay down his duties and come to Europe that spring: 'we could at once set about getting ready for the printers some of your literary work?'[139] Burr made the case that White required a disciple in case the worst happened: 'should anything happen ... the work must, like every such labor of love depend upon the chances of other men's leisure'.[140]

White ignored these invitations until early June, 1885, when he announced his planned resignation as President of Cornell and outlined plans to visit Europe and for his future publications – plans which would also involve Burr: 'Write me fully and carefully how all this strikes you, where in your judgement it would be well to begin, and where and in what field you would prefer to work with me. For I have always planned to make you my colleague in all this'.[141] Unfortunately, when Burr embraced his role as 'colleague' too eagerly, giving White his – apparently too honest – opinion on the amount of work yet to be done, White replied that 'the whole matter had perhaps better await our meeting'.[142] A lengthy letter in which Burr set out his views of history was more kindly received: 'I do not think that two men could agree more fully than we do on the whole subject ... I hope that we may be of use to each other' – again, still something less than a full partnership.[143]

---

[136] Burr to White. Zurich, 5 May 1886; Burr to White. Paris, 7 November 1885.
[137] Burr to White. Trier, 12 April 1886.   [138] Burr to White. Leipzig, 24 November 1884.
[139] Burr to White. Leipzig, 2 February 1885.
[140] White to Burr. Ithaca, NY, 26 January 1885; Burr to White. Leipzig, 12 February 1885.
[141] White to Burr. Ithaca, NY, 11 June 1885; White to Burr. Ithaca, NY, June 24, 1885.
[142] Burr to White. Zurich, 7 July 1885; White to Burr. Ithaca, NY, 22 July, 1885.
[143] Burr to White. Zurich, 10 July 1885; White to Burr. Ithaca, NY, 27 July 1885.

As the two men felt their way to sharing White's project, they also needed to carve out something that belonged to Burr. The student's original ideas for his doctoral dissertation – his 'Arbeit' – would have elaborated on and sustained his patron's research interests.[144] Burr, at first, had suggested two vast topics, 'the relation of the Universities to freedom of thought' and 'the struggle for the abolition of censure in Europe', that fit seamlessly within White's larger project.[145] Yet while White thoroughly approved of them ('I hardly know which I like best'), the student had settled on editing the Flade manuscript, which had come into White's possession in 1883 after Burr had spotted it in a Berlin old-book catalogue.[146] White's approval of Burr's new topic is telling: 'I do not see that your work need cross mine in any way. I have always intended to put that and other similar studies together in a book; but even in that case there would be no harm done to either of us'.[147] Burr was given access, but the terrain was White's already and remained so.

As the prospect of closer proximity became more real, it reawakened in Burr fears about his dependency on his patron and how that might affect their relationship. He expressed 'a horror of becoming, or seeming to become, in any sense, a parasite upon you', and he repeated his comment that 'so soon as you are through with me, I am ready even impatient, to be set adrift'. He insisted that his motivations were entirely selfless: 'only the love I bear you and the gratitude I owe you, added to the sincere conviction that if I can indeed help you, I shall be serving the world better than would be possible in my own little sphere, has led me so persistently to speak of your work as ours'.[148] White soothed Burr's anxieties by affirming their (near) equal partnership: 'I propose something like a partnership – at least something leading to that very directly. Your word "parasite" I do not like – there is nothing in our actual or possible relations corresponding to it'.[149] For his part, Burr, ashamed of 'the doubts that came to me', implicitly rejected this offer of equality: 'loneliness begets strange fears and fancies . . . I remain yours to command'.[150] The bundle of emotions on display in these letters is complex, and the men's inability to define their relationship is understandable: Burr's desire for White's proximity and his fear of rejection were clearly linked, but White's need to assert his higher status

---

[144] For the reference to 'the subject of my Arbeit', see Burr to White. Leipzig, 17 January 1885. White had similarly asked Burr about 'selecting your Fach or subject': White to Burr. Ithaca, NY, 24 November 1884.

[145] Burr to White. Leipzig, 8 December 1884.

[146] White to Burr. Ithaca, NY, 23 December 1884. For the history of the MS and White's acquisition of it, see the lengthy footnote in Burr, 'The Fate of Dietrich Flade', p. 191.

[147] White to Burr. Ithaca, NY, 26 January 1885.   [148] Burr to White. Zurich, 13 August 1885.

[149] White to Burr. Saratoga Springs, NY, 26 August 1885.

[150] Burr to White. Trier, 10 September 1585.

complicated a similar desire for closeness. When combined, these two sets of feelings generated a magnetic pulse that alternately attracted and repulsed.

White's arrival in Europe did not herald the dreamed-for partnership. Throughout White's tour of the continent, Burr variously acted as a baggage handler, as an apprentice and disciple, and as an amanuensis. Burr was entrusted with the care of the physical *Warfare of Science* manuscript along with the rest of White's trunks. In case anything happened while White was taking in the sights of Capri and Campania, he expressed the hope 'that if I do not complete them you will'.[151] White encouraged Burr to refute an article on Galileo written 'under Jesuit or at least priestly inspiration' as 'a good thing for the country and for yourself', which would later become a draft chapter for the *Warfare of Science* manuscript.[152] When Burr's time in Europe came to an end in September 1886, he promised White (who was still overseas) that 'what spare time I have shall be given to excerpting for the "Warfare of Science" such material as you have not already used'.[153]

Inevitably, Burr's witchcraft studies were also part of White's project and were similarly shaped by his relationship to his patron. The young American conceived of witchcraft in the same way his mentor conceived of all forms of false belief. Like other types of dogma, witchcraft belief existed only to be refuted as the absence or corruption of something good. While magic may be 'actual and universal', witchcraft was only ever 'a shadow, a nightmare . . . Less than five centuries saw its birth, its vigor, its decay'.[154] Burr's rather repetitive metaphors tellingly cast witchcraft belief as pale, perverse imitations easily defeated by the real thing. Witchcraft was a 'nightmare of Christian thought', 'the nightmare of a religion, the shadow of a dogma', and 'the shadow on the dial whose recession marks the upward course of the sun of civilization' – its decline marked progress.[155] These fundamentally Christian metaphors set up witchcraft's inevitable conquest at the hands of those scholars who let 'in the purer daylight'.[156] Although Burr was not alone in being primarily interested in opposition to the witch-hunt, both factors – witchcraft as the corruption of *something* else, to be refuted by *someone* else – helped locate witchcraft solidly within the larger *Warfare of Science* project, in which devout individuals fought

---

[151] White to Burr. Sorrento, 23 March 1886; Burr to White. Trier, 29 March 1886.

[152] White to Burr. Cannes, 11 January 1886; White to Burr. Cannes, 15 January 1886; Burr to White. Zurich, March 26, 1887[=8]. The article that outraged the two men was Glover, 'Rome and the Inquisitions'. Bainton reports that the Galileo chapter was intended for future editions of the *Warfare of Science* project: Bainton, 'His Life', p. 52.

[153] Burr to White. Ithaca, NY, 4 September 1886.

[154] George Lincoln Burr, 'The Literature of Witchcraft', p. 166.

[155] Burr, 'A Witch-Hunter in the Book-Shops', p. 294; Burr, 'The Literature of Witchcraft', p. 166; Robbins, *Witchcraft*, p. xiv.

[156] Burr, 'The Literature of Witchcraft', p. 187.

monstrous perversions of dogmatic religion.[157] As we have already seen in
Burr's reviews of Murray and Summers, for the remainder of his life Burr held
on to this view of witchcraft as a false perversion – a view which also helped to
relegate these beliefs to the past. After all, we wake up from a nightmare.

While these intellectual foundations remained unchanged – indeed, they
remained central to Burr's understanding of his own role and duty as a historian – his witchcraft studies also provided an avenue for his emancipation from
White. Upon his return from Europe, in his 1886 lecture on the Loos manuscript, Burr quelled his private doubts about Flade's worthy martyrdom.[158] Five
years later his attitude towards Flade had changed. In 'The Fate of Dietrich
Flade' (1891), he still mustered Martin Delrio's condemnation of Flade and
evidence from silence as best he could. He suggested in passing that the 'stout
denials' of one victim may have set Flade thinking, 'though there is little in the
record to suggest conscientious scruples on his part'.[159] A complaint by one of
the witch-hunters about the sluggishness of a nearby court could only apply to
Flade's – 'the only tribunal . . . he could have reason to complain [about] was
that of which Dietrich Flade was the head'.[160] Yet in the end, the evidence for
Flade's heroic opposition to the witch-hunt no longer stacked up. Burr admitted
that Flade 'was not a martyr – scarcely even a hero'.[161] Yet Burr could not give
up on Flade – and, indirectly, on White – entirely. Adopting a lower standard of
heroism he still found valour in the everyday: 'it is something to know that, even
in that most drearily doctrinaire of ages, there lived plodding men of affairs,
who, spite of dogma and of panic, clung to their common-sense and their
humanity, and with such firmness as was in them breasted the fate that came'.[162]

Upon reading Burr's 1891 article, the historian Henry Charles Lea (1825–
1909), an authority on the Spanish Inquisition but with an interest in witchcraft,
wrote to Burr to praise his 'exceeding thoroughness' as 'a matter of which not
only you but all American students of history have reason to be praised'.[163] This

---

[157] In 1904, Burr wrote to Lea that 'I still hope to have something to print in that field [witchcraft
history]; but what most interests me in it is the work of the opponents of the persecution':
Philadelphia, University of Pennsylvania, MS Coll. 111: Henry Charles Lea papers, Box 4,
Folder 209. Ithaca, NY, 26 February 1904.

James Bryce (later Viscount Bryce, 1838–1922), then British ambassador to Washington,
DC, heard Burr's paper on 'New England's Place in the History of Witchcraft' at the 1911
meeting of the American Antiquarian Society in Worcester, MA, and solicited a letter from Burr
on 'anybody who in the sixteenth or seventeenth century was wholly skeptical as to witchcraft
and the superstitions akin to it': Oxford, Bodleian Library, MS Bryce USA 12, fols. 116r–117v,
at 116r. Ithaca, NY, 3 October 1912.

[158] Burr, 'On the Loos Manuscript', pp. 149–50. Italics in the original.

[159] Burr, 'The Fate of Dietrich Flade', p. 199.   [160] Burr, 'The Fate of Dietrich Flade', p. 225.

[161] Burr, 'The Fate of Dietrich Flade', p. 232.   [162] Burr, 'The Fate of Dietrich Flade', p. 233.

[163] Philadelphia, University of Pennsylvania, MS Coll. 111: Henry Charles Lea papers, Box 4,
Folder 207. Philadelphia, 18 July, 1891.

compliment brings us to another difference between Burr and White. Burr's commitment to factual accuracy, as Bainton noted long ago, contrasted with his patron's 'hasty procedures' – or rather, to put it more accurately, with the latter's commitment to philosophical truth over 'surface facts', his concern with making 'the fundamental facts shine through the surface annals'.[164] 'The Fate of Dietrich Flade' offers a glimpse of how Burr attempted to resolve the tension between these opposing forces: by emphasizing humanity rather than reason. Tellingly, White continued to refer to Flade as a martyred opponent of the witch-hunt without Burr's careful caveats.[165] The triumph of the truth of facts over the truth of narrative in Burr's writings closely maps on to his gradually changing relationship with White. In the short term Burr's discovery of the Loos manuscript revealed an opponent of the witch-hunt whose bona fides could not be doubted.[166] Both White and Burr proved ready, as have more recent historians, to overlook Cornelius Loos's deep hostility (to be expected, perhaps, from a Catholic exile) towards Protestant heretics, whom he was more than happy to see burn.[167]

Burr's ambiguous attitude towards Flade reflects the fact that he could not escape White's orbit. Throughout 1886 and 1887 he had been desperate to avoid making a second European trip for White.[168] He described his first 1884–86 journey to Europe as his *Wanderjahre* – literally 'wander-years', but also a reference to the traditional German training of journeymen.[169] Having completed them, Burr sought to be a master in his own right. During his first stay he had kept up an exchange with a childhood sweetheart – known only from his diary as 'P.' – and was nearly engaged to her, but his straitened financial circumstances and the need to support his family made that impossible.[170] He also discovered that time and continued involvement with the *Warfare* project rebalanced his relationship with White. During his second stay in Europe, in

---

[164] Bainton, 'His Life', p. 52; White, 'On Studies in General History', p. 55.

[165] White, *Warfare*, vol. I, pp. 356–7; White, *Seven Great Statesmen*, p. 141.

[166] Burr, 'On the Loos Manuscript', p. 153.

[167] White, *Warfare*, vol. I, 356: 'He was a devoted churchman, and one of the most brilliant opponents of Protestantism, *but* he finally saw through the prevailing belief regarding occult powers, and in an evil hour for himself embodied his idea in a book entitled True and False Magic'. (Emphasis added) Burr, of course, had been more suspect: Burr, 'On the Loos Manuscript', p. 151. For an introduction to Cornelius Loos and his attempts to publish his *De vera et falsa magia*, see Rita Voltmer, 'Demonology and Anti-Demonology'. Efforts to publish the Loos manuscript have repeatedly failed. A German translation by the late Othon Scholer and revised by Luc Deitz is now finally forthcoming.

[168] Burr to White. Ithaca, NY, 1 August 1887: 'Let us first make one more effort to find somebody who can help you as well as I'.

[169] Burr, 'A Witch-Hunter in the Book-Shops', p. 296. I am grateful to Alison Rowlands for this insight.

[170] Bainton, 'His Life', pp. 36–7.

1887–88, Burr (supported by two assistants) worked extensively on *Warfare of Science* chapters on education, evolution, the antiquity of man, and comparative philology.[171] At that stage, with a post as history professor at Cornell in the offing, Burr became quite comfortable describing the project as belonging to them both. In January 1888 he was hard at work not only on White's education chapter but also on his doctoral dissertation and the lectures he would give at Cornell in the autumn: 'After all I feel more and more that, in the long run – as you have said yourself – our work is the same'.[172] Although White had long since stepped down from his roles at Cornell, in March Burr 'looked forward with impatience to a good time coming when you and I can divide up the nineteen Christian centuries among us after our own fashion, leaving to President Adams the history of institutions and to Professor Tuttle that of diplomacy, in which they most delight'.[173] In May he wrote to White that he understood their shared purpose: 'Now that I have grown to know how largely our work is one, I am no longer afraid of you and do not fail to see that what is best for me physically is best for us both and for the work'.[174] He also felt emboldened to correct White, at least in private and after 'long hesitation and painful struggle'. Even so, he told White, 'the choice lay only between <u>correcting you now</u> and <u>attacking you afterwards</u>'. (Burr's assertiveness only went so far, however. His attempt at correction ended with a profession of obedience. White could cable the word 'Insert!' and Burr would restore the original text.)[175]

A more important divergence between the erstwhile teacher and student than Burr's scruples about factual accuracy was the alternate, less fact-heavy theory of warfare that he put forward. In the same letter in which he corrected White's chapter, he also pushed the idea of publishing a *Warfare of Humanity*: 'I believe that Theology has too long been allowed to claim for itself a monopoly on the gentler impulses of human nature; and that, when the truth is known, the <u>heart</u> will be found to have had with theology as long and sharp a historic struggle for its rights as has the mind'.[176] In 1889, in a paper read at a meeting of the American Historical Association, Burr was more timid. He claimed that the 'delusion . . . faded before the advance of that more Christian spirit of mingled science and humanity which the world has too long stigmatized as rationalism'.[177] Yet over time humanity won out. In his 1891 sermon on 'The

---

[171] See e.g. Burr to White. London, 22 January 1888; Burr to White. Zurich, 16 March 1888.

[172] Burr to White. London, 22 January 1888.   [173] Burr to White. Zurich, 26 March 1888.

[174] Burr to White. Zurich, 5 May 1888.

[175] Burr to White. Ithaca, NY, 2 December 1888. Underlining in the original. The letter is partly excerpted in part in Bainton, 'His Life', 53–4.

[176] Burr to White. Ithaca, NY, 2 December 1888. Underlining in the original.

[177] Burr, 'The Literature of Witchcraft', p. 186.

Living Gospel' (mentioned earlier), Burr explicitly put his hope not in reason but in 'Christian kindliness': 'reason defended' witchcraft persecutions and despotism out of Scripture.[178] In a sermon, first delivered in 1905, Burr was still more explicit: 'Men sometimes tell us that what has brought us tolerance is only the growth of rationalism, the rise of the sciences'. Here, the reference to White is unmistakable. By contrast, his own studies taught Burr that 'the greatest scholars . . . were often, as they are to-day, the most intolerant of men. It was the men of loving hearts and of broad acquaintance'.[179] Progress should be ascribed 'less to any growth in knowledge than to that humanitarian trend, that new emphasis on conduct and on Christian kindliness, which has confessedly so marked the religious temper of our time'.[180] (In 1931, when Burr's students published a *festschrift* in honour of the fiftieth anniversary of his graduation from Cornell, they included chapters on Erasmus, Sebastian Castellio, and other 'humanitarians'. If White the Reformer resembled the scientists he championed, all these figures ended up rather resembling Burr.[181])

Burr's own war did not cause a break between the two men. In fact, White seems to have met Burr halfway, positioning his 1910 'Seven Great Statesmen' within 'the Warfare of *Humanity* with Unreason'.[182] In his obituary of White, Burr called the work 'a torso . . . He had hoped to parallel his "Warfare of Science" with as full a study of the great steps in the conflict with inhumanity and prejudice'.[183] The latter assertion might just be Burr (Figure 3) posthumously claiming White for his own project. Yet it may also point to another reason for their continued collaboration. Perhaps Burr, with his repeated insistence on the ultimate triumph of the 'kind of heart nurtured by the spirit of

---

[178] Burr, 'The Living Gospel', p. 239.

[179] Burr, 'Religious Progress', p. 313. Burr delivered the same text again in 1925, taking his audience 'back with me into the currents of that pre-war thinking' after 'a great war, with the conservative influence, the reactionary sequels, of all great wars, has thrown us back religiously whole decades': ibid., p. 309.

[180] Burr, 'Religious Progress', p. 314.

[181] See *Persecution and Liberty* (no editor is listed). The full titles of some of the contributions are already instructive: Wallace K. Ferguson, 'The Attitude of Erasmus toward Toleration'; Roland H. Bainton, 'Sebastian Castellio and the Toleration Controversy of the Sixteenth Century'; Edward M. Hulme, 'Lelio Sozzini's Confession of Faith'; and Lois Oliphant Gibbons, 'A Seventeenth Century Humanitarian: Hermann Löher'. Hulme's description of Sozzini (p. 211) can be easily applied to Burr: 'The narrative of his life is the story of a man seeking truth, pressing onward, quietly with reserves and reticences, to a religion that should satisfy at once the mind and the heart.' Bainton's conclusion about Castellio (p. 205) could summarize Burr's worldview: 'That which hinders us from seeing the truth is self-love, hate, prejudice, blind love, the desire for victory, which is ambition. The way to truth is identical with the mystic way to God. It consists in the crucifixion of the self.'

[182] Emphasis added. While 'humanity' replaces science, unreason remains. Burr was paid to correct the proofs of this work: Ogden (ed.), *The Diaries of Andrew D. White*, p. 426.

[183] Burr, 'Andrew Dickson White', p. 417.

Figure 3 George Lincoln Burr (ca. 1900). Image courtesy of Cornell University
Library.

Christianity', understood the ineffable religious mysticism at the heart of
White's project better than White himself ever did.[184]

Whatever Burr's qualms, when the completed two-volume edition of *Warfare
of Science* finally appeared in 1896, it was the product of two men and an
unequal teacher-student relationship. The result was that Burr's role in the
book's production was elided, but that he served a vital role as witness to
White's greatness. The publication of *Warfare* was accompanied by
a biographical 'Sketch' by Burr in *Popular Science Monthly*, the journal
which had printed many of its chapters as instalments.[185] Predictably, Burr
ended the portrait with a declaration of White's profound Christian faith: 'A
man of profoundly religious nature, impatient of irreverence of any kind, and
deeply attached to the Christian communion in which he was reared'.[186] The

---

[184] Burr to White. Ithaca, NY, 2 December 1888.

[185] For a sense of Burr's role in the revision of those articles, see Burr to White. Ithaca, NY,
16 December 1893; Burr to White. Ithaca, NY, 15 January 1894; and, especially, Burr to White.
Ithaca, NY, 26 February 1894, wherein Burr apologized for errors in the published text and
promised 'to read with more care'.

[186] Burr, 'Sketch of Andrew Dickson White', p. 556.

extent of Burr's contributions to the final text is impossible to determine, but it was profound.[187] Burr modestly noted that White 'has known how to use the aid from time to time of sundry helpers' in the gathering of material but claimed 'that in the digestion and interpretation of his materials no other hand was ever given a part'.[188] Burr thus also effaced his own role, at least partly because he privately continued to push White towards the warfare of humanity instead. Although in the preface of *Warfare of Science* White thanked Burr 'first and above all' for his 'contributions, suggestions, criticisms, and cautions', with the exception of Bainton's 1943 short life of Burr – where few scholars of White would ever think to look – his role in its composition has been completely forgotten.[189] Burr carried out his role as White's witness without fail until his death. As late as 1932, at a luncheon that honoured the centenary of White's birth, he gave a 'glowing tribute' to the sole 'builder' of Cornell University.[190]

5 Meditations on Masculinity

So far we have charted the bonds that tied Burr to White, but, as already indicated, the connections that both men forged with past historical figures, especially Loos and Flade, were at least as important for their scholarship. When Burr first reached Trier, he found a room 'on the very street where Dr Flade used to live'. He also attempted a 'pilgrimage' to the grave of yet another Trier witchcraft sceptic, the Jesuit Friedrich Spee.[191] (Burr would later describe him as a 'saint and martyr by a higher canonization than that of the Church'.[192]) While working 'alone in the evening twilight' in Trier's former Jesuit library, he was conscious of being watched by the portrait of 'gentle Friedrich von Spee' (and by some less hospitable Electors): 'Friedrich v. Spee, indeed, sleeps scarce twenty yards away in the old crypt. I can almost fancy him shudder in his grave as I turn the leaves of these bloody old witchcraft records'.[193] The parallels between White and Burr on the one hand, and Flade and Loos on the other, really were unmistakable. Flade had been the rector or 'University President' of the University of Trier, just as White had been at Cornell.[194] Loos was described as a 'young college professor', just when Burr took up his first instructorship at Cornell.[195] (In reality, Loos would have been in his

---

[187] See also Bainton, 'His Life', p. 52. Burr's papers at Cornell contain more than two boxes of material related to the Warfare of Science project: Ithaca, NY, Cornell University Rare and Manuscript Collections, George Lincoln Burr Papers: Box 29 (folders 20 and 21 only), Box 30, and Box 31.

[188] Burr, 'Sketch of Andrew Dickson White', p. 556.   [189] White, *Warfare*, vol. I, p. x.

[190] 'Centenary of Birth of Dr. Andrew White Celebrated by Alumni'; 'Excerpt from Prof. Burr's Speech'.

[191] Burr to White. Trier, 31 August 1885.   [192] Burr, 'The Literature of Witchcraft', p. 186.

[193] Burr to White. Trier, 30 March 1886.   [194] Burr, 'On the Loos Manuscript', p. 149.

[195] Adams, 'A Manuscript and a Man'.

late forties or early fifties when he composed the discovered witchcraft manuscript, and he never seems to have had any academic employment.)

White's *Seven Great Statesmen* similarly shows that the author so identified with his subjects and so embodied the values he ascribed to them that he appeared to be their reincarnation.[196] Paolo Sarpi was neither Catholic nor Protestant, but Christian: 'a thoughtful, quiet scholar – large-minded and tolerant', who 'must have' loathed, among others, the German Reformer Benedict Carpzov who 'had sent witches to the scaffold by the thousands'.[197] Hugo Grotius, like White, 'steered clear of the quicksands of useless scholarship, which had engulfed so many strong men of his time. The zeal of learned men in that period was largely given to knowing things not worth knowing, to discussing things not worth discussing, to proving things not worth proving'.[198] Yet of the seven figures, White probably identified most with Christian Thomasius, who had been one of the first rectors of the University of Halle (Figure 1). If Cornell had been a 'godless institution' in the eyes of its critics, then Halle had been a 'hellish' (*höllisches*) one.[199] White suggested that Thomasius, a late and (frankly) rather timid critic of the witch-hunt, might have been haunted by 'remembrances of the fate of many who had made a similar fight' – especially the fate of Flade, 'like him an eminent jurist and a university professor'.[200]

That White and Burr identified with their historical subjects, then, is readily apparent. Theirs was also firmly a history of Great Men, their admiration for some women (notably, 'Saint' Florence Nightingale) notwithstanding.[201] Yet the extent to which these factors – and their masculine identities – shaped their scholarship may be less obvious. At first glance the evidence for any misogynistic attitudes may seem less than clear-cut. White favoured the admission of women to Cornell University, but (as we shall see) for reasons that were less than egalitarian.[202] Unlike Burr, who remained steadfastly opposed to women's suffrage, White voted ('with many misgivings', he told his diary) in favour of the Nineteenth Amendment.[203] Burr, who in his youth composed a satire

---

[196] I have taken the idea 'that virtues are the distinctive marks of scholarly personae' from Paul, 'What Is a Scholarly Persona?', esp. p. 350.

[197] White, *Seven Great Statesmen*, p. 48.   [198] White, *Seven Great Statesmen*, p. 58.

[199] White, *Seven Great Statesmen*, p. 133.

[200] White, *Seven Great Statesmen*, p. 146. See also the reference to the 'ex-Rector of [Trier's] University' on p. 141.

[201] White, *Warfare* (1876), p. 150. White even commissioned a stained-glass window of Nightingale for Cornell's Sage Chapel from a London artist: Burr to White. London, 1 February 1888. Nightingale did not personify manly virtues. She was chosen because she was 'fitted to take a place among the sweet-souled, helpful-handed women of our own day whose memorials sanctify those walls': Burr, 'The Living Gospel', p. 239.

[202] Haines, 'For Honor and Alma Mater'.

[203] Ogden (ed.), *The Diaries of Andrew D. White*, p. 466 (2 November 1915); Bainton, 'His Life', p. 127.

entitled 'Our First Woman President', had warm relationships with female doctoral students – one of whom would edit a posthumous collection of his writings.[204] None of them, however, ended up in academic employment, nor did Burr appear to expect them to.

If this does not seem overwhelmingly misogynistic, then that is precisely what historians of scholarly masculinity have taught us to expect. The professionalization of historical research in the nineteenth century was a process of transforming the historian into a figure who was invisible and objective, yet also gendered male, *because* objectivity and professionalism were seen as masculine, as defined against feminine 'amateurism'.[205] Historical seminars and archives were male spaces, the new practices that accompanied them 'proposed a masculine identity worthy of and equal to the arduous quest for objectivity'.[206] Yet this rhetoric of universality did more than simply identify itself against femininity: it also subsumed the feminine as a lesser subcategory. As Joan Wallach Scott put it, 'the feminine was but a particular instance; the masculine a universal signifier'.[207] Cornell University's early admission of women (especially early when compared to its more established Ivy League competitors) did not challenge the masculine universalist paradigm: the presence of women was meant to underwrite it, as we shall see.[208]

It will come as no surprise that White's conception of history was thoroughly masculine from the outset. In his first magazine article he concluded that the 'contemplation of the bearing of increased liberty on increased virtue, and of struggles of great good men with great bad men, strengthens a man's heart. . . . This is that higher discipline which gives mental discipline its worth; this repays all discouragement among old books – all buffeting among rugged men'.[209] By contrast, students at America's denominational colleges graduated with, at best, 'clerically emasculated knowledge of the most careful modern thought'.[210] Small incidents characterize White's and Burr's 'masculine' attitudes just as much. At the 1885 American Historical Association meeting, White encountered a 'crankish' female member but he 'quickly got rid of her'.[211] In a letter to White, Burr expressed his 'amazement and indignation' that 'the important article' on Galileo in the *Encyclopaedia Britannica* 'had been entrusted to

---

[204] Bainton, 'His Life', pp. 9, 127.   [205] See, in particular, Smith, *The Gender of History*.

[206] Smith, *The Gender of History*, p. 105; see also Smith, 'Gender and the Practices of Scientific History'.

[207] Scott, *Gender and the Politics of History*, p. 183.

[208] For a study of the admission of women at Harvard, Yale, and Princeton, see Malkiel, *"Keep the Damned Women Out"*.

[209] White, 'Glimpses of Universal History', p. 427.   [210] White, *Warfare* (1876), p. 137.

[211] Ogden (ed.), *The Diaries of Andrew D. White*, p. 247.

a woman'.[212] White admired Lecky's historical scholarship because, he told Burr, 'the reading of history of that sort makes not pedants but men'.[213] What the two scholars objected to was the limited agency given to the (male) sceptics in Lecky's witchcraft chapter.[214]

White and Burr may have felt a still greater need to assert the masculinity of their project because it strayed from the ideals of historical objectivity espoused by their peers. White used decidedly gendered language to discredit the supposed prophet of scientific objectivity, Leopold von Ranke. In his *Autobiography* White mocked Ranke, whose lectures he had attended in his youth, by feminizing him: 'half a dozen students crowding around his desk, listening as priests might listen to the sibyl on her tripod'.[215] According to Burr, White considered 'the trend of the German method toward minute research ... academic and devitalizing'.[216] But the 'masculinity' of White's historical project finds its greatest expression in the metaphor that was at its heart – and historians of science have, to my knowledge, strangely never commented on it. As Michael Kimmel has noted, 'all wars ... are meditations on masculinity'.[217] For White, the war of the scientists far excelled that of the soldiers. The warfare of science had seen 'warriors' engaged in 'fiercer' battles and 'more persistent' sieges than 'the comparatively petty warfares of Alexander, or Caesar, or Napoleon'.[218]

White's preoccupation with masculinity was also evident in the policies he pursued at Cornell. He was proud of the 'strong men' he had recruited to teach at Cornell – with Burr as the prime example within the history department – and rejected one job applicant because he was insufficiently manly, writing to his deputy that he preferred 'thoroughbreds' and wished to have 'a

---

[212] Burr to White. London, 18 February 1886.

[213] White to Burr. Ithaca, NY, 13 August 1885. Underlining in the original manuscript.

[214] Burr, 'The Literature of Witchcraft', p. 181.

[215] White, *Autobiography*, vol. I, p. 139, which goes on to comment that Ranke 'had a habit of becoming so absorbed in his subject, as to slide down in his chair, hold his finger up toward the ceiling, and then, with his eye fastened on the tip of it, to go mumbling through a kind of rhapsody'. The somewhat less gendered parallel description in White's diary ('The great historian during most of his hour lay sprawled out in his chair looking upwards and talking to himself, now quickly, now slowly, now loud, now soft!') is cited in Smith's study: Ogden (ed.), *The Diaries of Andrew D. White*, p. 100 (October 30, 1855); Smith, *The Gender of History*, p. 106.

[216] Hewett, *Cornell University*, vol. II, p. 102. According to Bainton, 'His Life', p. 122, this section on the teaching of history was written by Burr 'because of a wish to redress a slight to Andrew Dickson White in the first volume'.

[217] Kimmel, *Manhood in America*, p. 72.

[218] See e.g. the description of Columbus as 'the next warrior': White, 'The Battle-Fields of Science'. In his lecture on 'The Age of Discovery', p. 29 (Andrew Dickson White Papers, Reel 140, p. 24), White also emphasized how Columbus 'developed his natural manliness and Godliness'.

Faculty as free as possible from the influence of half way men'.[219] While White's intellectualized conception of masculinity – for very personal reasons – did not fully align with those of nineteenth-century America, he embraced the military drilling made compulsory for Cornell men by the Morrill Land Grant.[220] He erected 'one of the largest gymnasiums in the country' for their use and hired an 'experienced gymnast' to train them.[221] The male students slept in dormitories and arose at 5AM in summer and 5:30AM in winter.[222] White was pleased when a group of Cornell students was victorious over Harvard and Yale during an 1875 boat race, and was especially delighted by the 'manly qualities which they showed in the hour of triumph'.[223] A young Burr fully understood what made Cornell different: where 'other colleges strive to make boys pious', he wrote in a student essay, 'Cornell [strives] to make them manly'.[224] Inevitably, manhood – and Burr's need to assert it – also helps to account for Burr's later and partial quest for independence.

Even Cornell's admission of women had the manliness of the men foremost in mind. White claimed that their admission would make the men 'more manly' and the women 'more womanly' (as his mother had told him it would).[225] In his report to the Trustees, White stressed that the admission of women would especially advantage men:

> The greatest aid which could be rendered to smooth the way for any noble thinkers who are to march through the future, would be to increase the number of women who, by an education which has caught something from manly methods, are prevented from … throwing themselves hysterically across their pathway.[226]

The passage at once highlights the masculinity of universal ideals and the dangers posed by women, while in effect also incorporating them in a subservient position – evidently, they could never be ranked among the 'noble thinkers'. White further claimed that 'the fetichisms and superstitions of the world are bolstered up mainly by women'.[227] Needless to say, this belief in the superstitious nature of women also shaped White's view of the past. The weapons used by the opponents of scientists – the epithets 'Infidel' and

---

[219] White, *Autobiography*, vol. I, p. 381; White to William Channing Russell. Long Branch, NJ, 18 August 1870.

[220] Haines, 'For Honor and Alma Mater', 26.

[221] White (ed.), *'What Profession Shall I Choose and How Shall I Fit Myself or It?'*, p. 53. The women were provided with 'a smaller but well-equipped gymnasium'.

[222] Altschuler, *Andrew D. White*, pp. 78–9.   [223] White, *Autobiography*, vol. I, p. 353.

[224] Cited in Bainton, 'His Life', p. 16.   [225] White, *Autobiography*, vol. I, pp. 397–8, 400.

[226] White, *Report Submitted to the Trustees of Cornell University*, p. 36.

[227] White, *Report*, p. 36.

'Atheist' – harmed men only indirectly through their families: 'They go to the
heart of loving women: they alienate dear children; they injure the man after life
is ended, for they leave poisoned wounds in the hearts of those who loved him
best – fears for his eternal happiness, dread of the Divine displeasure'.[228]
Fortunately, the weapons have since lost some of their edge: 'though often
effective in scaring women, [they] are somewhat blunted'.[229]

This central preoccupation with masculinity sustained White's identity,
his reforming project, and his scholarship. Unsurprisingly, then, in White's
view, women, including those accused of witchcraft, shared responsibility
for the witch-hunt with the male scholastics and inquisitors who pursued
them. White suggested that no other cause had so often given rise to witch-
hunts 'as the alleged bewitchment of some poor mad or foolish or hysterical
creature. ... Well-authenticated, though rarer than is often believed, were
the cases where crazed women voluntarily accused themselves of this
impossible crime'.[230] White cited a German psychiatrist who declared
that their recorded conversations were 'exactly like those familiar to him
in our modern lunatic asylums'.[231] Convents, in particular, were 'breeding-
beds' of the disease.[232] White concluded that 'one evidence of Satanic
intercourse with mankind especially, on which for many generations theologians had laid peculiar stress, and for which they had condemned scores
of little girls and hundreds of old women to a most cruel death, was found
to be nothing more than one of the many results of hysteria'.[233] White thus
outlined an unhealthy relationship between *seemingly* learned clerics and
their enabling female victims, which was interrupted by heroic male
opponents:

> in the midst of demonstrations of demoniacal possession by the most eminent
> theologians and judges, who sat in their robes and *looked* wise, while women,
> shrieking, praying, and blaspheming, were put to the torture, a man arose who
> dared to protest effectively that some of the persons thus charged might be
> simply insane; and this man was [the witchcraft sceptic] John Wier [or
> Weyer], of Cleves.[234]

If nineteenth-century American men defined their masculinity primarily in
relation to each other, then White's representation of the conflict between
theologians and sceptics reflects these attitudes.[235]

Burr took issue with White on the culpability of supposedly hysterical
victims. The caveat 'though rarer than is often believed' may well be by his

---

[228] White, 'The Battle-Fields of Science'.   [229] White, 'The Battle-Fields of Science'.
[230] White, *Warfare*, vol. II, p. 118.   [231] White, *Warfare*, vol. II, p. 118.
[232] White, *Warfare*, vol. II, p. 121.   [233] White, *Warfare*, vol. II, p. 125.
[234] White, *Warfare*, vol. II, p. 122. Emphasis added.   [235] Kimmel, *Manhood in America*.

hand (we know he inserted others.) Yet he only disagreed because the female victims were *superfluous*. In a letter to White, he explained that torture was 'the sufficient explanation of the witch-confessions'. In fact, the 'very few' cases of insanity had been used by modern theologians (that is, by White and Burr's male opponents) 'who would fain exculpate religion by throwing the blame on the victims themselves'. Like White, Burr saw the witch-hunt as a conflict between male elites: 'Weyer [Wier] . . . sought to save the witches by making them out demented. And the persecutors, who fought him tooth and nail on this point, saw that this was to undermine their whole position'.[236]

The witch-hunt, then, was a battle between rival masculinities. Burr took issue with Lecky's assessment of the sceptics: 'the opponents of the persecution seem to me neither so few nor so feeble as one might infer from the pages of Mr. Lecky'.[237] In his first lecture on the Loos manuscript, he ranked the sceptics as 'often the most learned and honored [men] of their respective communities', although for the most part too frightened to speak up. Wier was 'the first man who dare to raise his voice'; Loos was the 'next man . . . who dared to stand out boldly'.[238] The victims of the witch-hunt received little attention. Burr asked his audience to imagine those imprisoned in a witch-tower. His description began with a 'fair' maiden – 'her conscience black with tortured lies that blast her own fair name'. But Burr quickly moved on to the male prisoners: an imprisoned village pastor, 'touched by the sufferings of his people into questioning whether the Devil could really do all that was ascribed to him'; before dwelling, as already noted, on Flade himself: 'a man of presence and dignity, whose chain of gold points to exalted rank . . . who was brought into suspicion because as a judge he began to doubt whether *all* the witches were guilty of *all* the crimes laid to their charge'.[239] For Burr, the female victims of the witch-hunt were innocent but scarcely ever worthy of attention, while male victims were their heroic defenders, falsely accused of witchcraft as a result.

Scholarly masculinity not only shaped how the two historians understood the witch-hunt; the entire *Warfare of Science* thesis was effectively a conflict between rival versions of manhood. White generally emphasized the laziness of mind and body of those who opposed his heroes who 'patiently, fearlessly, and reverently devote themselves to the search for truth as truth'.[240] These were 'older theologians, who since their youth have learned nothing and forgotten nothing, sundry professors who do not wish to rewrite their lectures'.[241] They

---

[236] Burr to White. Ithaca, NY, 2 December 1888. Underlining in the original.
[237] Burr, 'The Literature of Witchcraft', p. 181.   [238] Burr, 'On the Loos Manuscript', p. 150.
[239] Burr, 'On the Loos Manuscript', pp. 149–50. Italics in the original.
[240] White, *Warfare of Science*, vol. I, p. 248.
[241] White, *Warfare of Science*, vol. I, pp. 318–19.

also took fright easily,[242] and engaged in 'unmanly' behaviour, such as attacking Galileo when he was prevented from responding.[243] Ideas and expressions, too, were either manly or sterile and emasculating: 'Which is the more likely to strengthen Christianity', White asked rhetorically: 'a large, manly, honest, fearless utterance' or 'hair-splitting sophistries, bearing in their every line the germs of failure?'[244] Even Germany could be represented in anthropomorphized form as 'a strong, sound man building up his whole higher nature in struggling with obstacles and dangers'.[245]

If, as argued above, the *Warfare of Science* was impelled by White's own identity as a reformer, then it was also in part the product of his own idiosyncratic conception of manhood. As a young professor at the University of Michigan, White had sent 'to the field the young manhood of the North', equipped with John Lothrop Motley's three-volume *The Rise of the Dutch Republic* (although, characteristically, he did his utmost to avoid military service himself).[246] While White approved of physical exertion for others, the version of masculinity articulated in his writings stressed the superiority of the warfare of the mind, which he himself happened to embody. The very opposite of the then dominant 'self-made man', White was free from the necessity of hard work.[247] Perhaps paradoxically, his weak physical condition established his efforts as strenuous and at the same time justified leisure – his many European vacations were legitimated by the need to recover his health. In his obituary of White, Burr claimed that although White had 'never [been] in the most robust of health, a careful regimen made possible for him an amount of work that would have staggered many a stronger man'.[248] Accordingly, *Warfare of Science* was completed 'under many difficulties', which included not only many public duties but also the fact that White was 'obliged from time to time to throw off by travel the effects of overwork'.[249] White's obsession with over-exertion also enveloped Burr – the teacher was continuously anxious that his pupil was physically exhausting himself during

---

[242] White, *Warfare of Science*, vol. I, p. 91.

[243] White, *Warfare of Science*, vol. I, p. 138. Note also the example of Archbishop Archibald Tait, deemed too timid a supporter of science: 'manly as he was, he was somewhat more cautious in this matter than those who most revere his memory could now wish': ibid., vol. II, p. 356.

[244] White, *Warfare of Science*, vol. I, p. 247.   [245] White, 'The New Germany', p. 207.

[246] Burr, 'Sketch of Andrew Dickson White', p. 551; White, *Autobiography*, vol. I, p. 87; Altschuler, *Andrew D. White*, p. 45.

[247] As the *New York Times* would note in its obituary, White's inheritance enabled him 'to be free from financial cares all his life and made possible many of his services which would have been beyond the reach of a man who had to work for a living'; 'Dr A.D. White dies'.

[248] Burr, 'Andrew Dickson White', p. 418. I am grateful to Anthony Grafton for pointing this striking preoccupation with health and overwork out to me.

[249] White, *Warfare*, vol. I, pp. ix–x.

his trips to Europe.[250] White's extensive overseas travels appear to indulge in the same form of escapism that dominated nineteenth-century American manhood. Yet where the typical white American male escaped West when responsibilities grew too much, White, 'breaking beneath his grief' after the death of his first wife, went to Europe.[251] White's health and status thus helped him embody the very conception of heroic intellectual manhood that he had idealized.

6 Reflections

This study has shown that there is room for – indeed, a deep need for – a type of historiography that moves beyond seeing historians as products of their time. White and Burr's letters and writings demonstrate the importance of paying close attention to the specific personal, individual circumstances in which historical scholarship is produced. Historians were humans too, and their concerns did more than reflect the times in which they lived. The wars which White and Burr waged, whether for science or humanity, do not fit the large historiographical frameworks – the 'conflict' thesis in history of science, the 'rationalist' paradigm for witchcraft history, the American interpretation of Rankean 'objectivity' – which were supposed to contain them. White's *Warfare of Science* was far from an anti-religious screed, but part of a project of religious reform with scientists in the role of religious reformers, who were accused of witchcraft (and much else) by their bigoted opponents. Burr's witchcraft sceptics were motivated less by right reason and the mind, and more by compassion and the heart. Neither was pursuing scientific objectivity; history for both was a moral science. The scholarship of both men, then, was the product of their identities. (Identity may be a more useful concept here than 'scholarly persona' because their identities – White the Reformer, Burr the Disciple and Humanitarian – were ultimately not about scholarship and were more than mere personae.) White and Burr were defined, in part, by shared duties, debts, and obligations, and their identities changed, along with their writings, as their relationship evolved from that of teacher and apprentice to something more equal. Their writings and relationship were also imbued with the need to define, protect, and assert their manhood.

---

[250] See, for instance, White to Burr. Ithaca, NY, 25 August 1884 (which expresses 'some fears that you will overdo it at Göttingen'), and White to Burr. Cambridge, 25 November 1885 ('I earnestly hope that your silence is not caused by illness; your statement regarding sleeplessness caused by work has made me rather nervous regarding you'). Concerns by White for Burr overburdening himself continued to surface during later trips to Europe: White to Burr. Ithaca, NY, 7 May 1888; White to Burr. Ithaca, NY, 25 June 1896.

[251] Burr, 'Sketch of Andrew Dickson White', p. 555. For the importance of escapism to nineteenth-century American manhood, see Kimmel, *Manhood in America*, chap. 2.

This Element was never intended as an exposé. It is neither a *j'accuse* or a *j'excuse*. It would be facile and wrong to conclude that White and Burr deserve our attention even less now that their 'faults' are laid bare. Indeed, the purpose has been the reverse. For starters, there remains much that is of value in Burr's scholarship – it is based on an impressive amount of archival research and reading.[252] More importantly, like White and Burr, we are human too. These two authors may inspire 'moral reflection' on contemporary models of historical scholarship, especially at a time when historical writing, with the rise of public history and impact case studies, is again meant to have societal impact.[253] Study of their project of activist history brings out some of the tensions within the project of history writing itself. The need to profess or appear to be objective often conflicts with our often very personal motivations for choosing our research topics, and with the morally charged mission to recover lost voices from the past – in short, with our humanity. Later generations of historians may see our debts, motivations, and blind spots more clearly than we do, but we ourselves should also do our best acknowledge them; the study of our predecessors may help us identify them. If the present Element is any guide, such study will show that historians cannot be reduced to products of their time and place, as historiography all too often does. Historians are also the product of relationships with others in the present and in the past. We should be conscious of such debts.

We should also not lose sight of the fact that history writing remains an incremental process. The unconscious assumptions and explicit aims of White and Burr's scholarship have left their mark on the later historiography, whether we are aware of them or not. This impact is most easily identified in witchcraft historiography, perhaps because, as a field of historical research, it has been relatively unreflective about its own past.[254] Perhaps the greatest paradox of White and Burr's scholarship is its impact on the study of male witches. Within their warfare framework, in which genders had clearly assigned roles, male witches were an anomaly that needed to be explained away. Perhaps the most important reason, then, why White and Burr continued to consider Flade a martyr was that they could not conceive of an elite male, so much like

---

[252] Voltmer, '"Germany's First "Superhunt"?', p. 229. Voltmer dedicated this chapter to Burr's memory. See also Voltmer's account of Burr's stay in Trier, which includes useful information on Trier and the Stadtbibliothek where Burr discovered the manuscript: Voltmer, 'Ein Amerikaner in Trier'.

[253] For the importance of such 'moral reflection', see also Paul, 'Sources of the Self'.

[254] Fudge, 'Traditions and Trajectories', p. 488, opens with the advice to ignore everything written before the 1960s, commenting that 'basic flaws in historical methodology crept into the early period of writing on the subject. Happily, these deficiencies were largely reversed from the 1970s'.

themselves, to have been a *passive* victim. He had to have been an opponent of the hunt, he had to have had agency. When in 1897 Burr published a – still valuable – selection of sources on the witch-hunt these included fragments from the Flade and Loos manuscripts, but they also introduced a third elite male witch: the mayor of Bamberg, Johannes Junius.[255] Thus explained away as sceptics and opponents, male witches did not receive scholarly attention until the early 2000s.[256] Laura Apps and Andrew Gow, in their groundbreaking study of male witches, attribute the exclusion of male witches from the historiography to 'active processes and assumptions', including 'a tacit agreement' between feminist and 'non-feminist' historians that they are 'neither as interesting nor as important as female witches and, furthermore, that they are not "proper" witches'.[257] Scholarly masculinity helped to create this blind spot.

Other consequences of the warfare framework had, to some extent, become apparent in Burr's own lifetime. In addition to taking on Murray and Summers across the pond, Burr also faced an opponent closer to home, in the form of the Harvard professor George Lyman Kittredge (1860–1941). Kittredge's challenge showed just how much Burr identified himself – whether in defence of Science or Humanity – with the sceptics he studied and how much he had invested emotionally in their righteousness. Where Burr blamed scholastic theology and male elites for the witch-hunt, Kittredge – whose work would inspire Keith Thomas – placed responsibility 'with the neighborhood or community', and he provocatively discussed 'the terrible prosecution in Trier toward the close of the sixteenth century' as 'a case in point'.[258] The Harvard professor emphasized fears of *maleficium*, 'the working of harm to the bodies and goods of one's fellow-men', as 'the essential element in witchcraft' and concluded that Burr had 'over-emphasize[d] the learned or literary side of the question'.[259] The normally mild-mannered Burr was still more upset by the claim that witchcraft belief was not only universal in the seventeenth century, 'even among the elite', but that it 'was no more discreditable to a man's head or heart than it was to believe in spontaneous generation or to be ignorant of the germ theory of disease'.[260] Burr claimed that Kittredge's conclusions were 'contradictory of what my own lifelong study in this field has seemed to teach' and 'so much more generous to our ancestors than

---

[255] Burr (ed.), *The Witch-Persecutions*, pp. 13–18, 23–8.

[256] Apps and Gow, *Male Witches in Early Modern Europe*; Schulte, *Man as Witch*; Rowlands (ed.), *Witchcraft and Masculinities in Early Modern Europe*.

[257] Apps and Gow, *Male Witches in Early Modern Europe*, pp. 26, 29.

[258] Kittredge, *Notes on Witchcraft*, p. 46. See also thesis no. 9 (on p. 66): 'The responsibility for any witch prosecution rests primarily on the community or neighborhood as a whole, not on the judge or the jury'. Ronald Hutton is right to describe Kittredge as 'unusual' and place White and Kittredge on opposing sides of a spectrum of attitudes, but he still overstates the consensus between the Harvard and Cornell scholars: Hutton, *The Triumph of the Moon*, pp. 133–4.

[259] Kittredge, *Notes on Witchcraft*, p. 5.   [260] Kittredge, *Notes on Witchcraft*, p. 66.

I can find it in my conscience to deem fair'.[261] Despite Kittredge's intervention, or indeed later ones, historians have continued to identify with witchcraft sceptics. A German society still awards the Friedrich Spee prize for best work in witchcraft history, without recognition that Spee – like Loos before him – fought heresy as fervently as others fought witchcraft.[262] While historians of science have long exposed the at times esoteric thought that underpinned the work of early scientists, similar studies of witchcraft sceptics would again wait until the twenty-first century.[263]

Military events proved an even greater shock, especially to White's warfare thesis, and demonstrated that progress was not, in the end, inevitable. Germany's invasion of neutral Belgium in 1914 destroyed its role as the Promised Land that had matched White's hopes for the future more than his own country. If facts had always been of secondary importance to White, German aggression simply could not be overlooked. In his diary he wrote that 'violating [the] neutrality of Belgium seems the unpardonable sin – and to these must be added dropping bombs into unfortified cities and killing women and children'.[264] In his 1905 *Autobiography* White had devoted an elegiac chapter to his personal reminiscences of Emperor William II whom he had known as US ambassador, and he was now forced to eat his own words.[265] The impact of White's positive view of Germany on witchcraft historiography was thus unintentional and profound. When White used Germany's role in the witch-hunt to illustrate the progress the country had made, he could not have foreseen that two World Wars would cause the same link to be used to illustrate the precise opposite: Germany as a home of irrational cruelty. British historians of the 1960s and 1970s, who had fought in World War II, would emphasize it.[266]

---

[261] Burr, 'New England's Place in the History of Witchcraft', p. 353.

[262] Kemper, 'Frank Sobiech Erhält den Preis des Paderborner Geschichtsvereins'.

[263] For studies of witchcraft sceptics, see Valente, *Johann Wier* (a revised English translation is forthcoming); Almond, *England's First Demonologist*; Hoorens, *Een ketterse arts voor de heksen*. Nevertheless, praise for witchcraft sceptics has by no means ceased. See, for instance, the attempt to place Spee among the 'Kämpfer für die Menschenrechte' (Fighters for Human Rights): Franz, 'Antonius Hovaeus, Cornelius Loos und Friedrich Spee', p. 132, and the examples under n. 59.

[264] Ogden (ed.), *The Diaries of Andrew D. White*, p. 458 (26 August 1914). See also the entry 4 April 1915 (p. 462): 'I can no longer sympathize with the Germans – strong as my leanings in that direction were. They seem determined to trample on all the best secured rights of nations'.

[265] White, *Autobiography*, vol. II, chap. XLIV ('My Recollections of William II – 1879–1903'); Altschuler, *Andrew D. White*, pp. 281–5.

[266] Trevor-Roper compared the witchcraft 'mythology' built up by inquisitors to 'the world-wide conspiracy of the Elders of Zion' created by anti-Semites: Trevor-Roper, *The European Witch-Craze*, pp. 92, 107; Cohn declared 'the great witch-hunt ... a supreme example of massive killing of innocent people by a bureaucracy ... Until our own century, the operation and consequences of demonization have never been more horrifyingly displayed': Cohn, *Europe's Inner Demons*, p. 233.

Refuting the connection and the implicit attack on Germany it entails seems, at times, to be the main aim of Germany's most prominent witchcraft historian.[267]

Study of past witchcraft historians, then, helps us explain why some aspects (male witches) have been overlooked, why others loom particularly large (Germany and its supposed lack of modernity), and why still others really do appear to be evergreens, reflecting the deeply felt need for heroes in history. The popularity of the early modern witch-hunt as a subject of study and appropriation by the present forms part of this wider legacy as well, pointing to the continued need for witchcraft's pastness and the need for that past to have meaning. Admiration of witchcraft sceptics may also help us to more easily perceive the appeal of the broader warfare thesis, because it stems from that same demand that history is not, to quote a young White, 'a mere game at cross-purposes, a careless whirl'. Of course, the past does not need to be a record of progress for it to have meaning. Yet progress seems what the present again demands. Already in 2004, Sam Harris, one of the so-called New Atheists, revived the old story of Dietrich Flade's heroism to underscore the evil that is religion.[268] While this movement may have lost momentum of late, the positive reception by scientists and the greater public of a 2020 biography of Galileo, with the fitting title *Galileo and the Science Deniers*, suggests that progress narratives are undergoing an urgent revival. (As the cover of that book screams, '400 years later [Galileo's] message and mission are as important as ever'.)[269] These returning narratives contain deeper truths about the present: they reveal how progress is seen as imperilled and in need of reinforcement, both real and rhetorical, and in need of warriors, old and new. The boundaries between the past and the present remain blurred, despite our efforts to keep the past as past. In short, more introspection may do us good. At the very least we should not forget that in their wars for progress White and Burr were roundly defeated. Whatever we do or do not do, we can be sure that future historians will have much to say about us.

---

[267] e.g. 'Germanophobia does not make more sense than a stereotyping hatred of any other linguistic or ethnic group': Wolfgang Behringer, 'Germany', p. 417. See also Behringer, 'Witchcraft Studies in Austria, Germany and Switzerland', pp. 84–5.

[268] See the refutation in Johnstone, *The New Atheism, Myth, and History*, esp. pp. 161–8.

[269] Livio, *Galileo and the Science Deniers*.

Bibliography

Manuscripts

Herman Paul, 'Sources of the Self: Scholarly Personae as Repertoires of Scholarly Selfhood', *BMGN - Low Countries Historical Review*, 131, no. 4 (2016), 135–154. https://doi.org/10.18352/bmgn-lchr.10268

Ithaca, NY, Cornell University Rare and Manuscript Collections
  Andrew Dickson White papers, 1832–1919 [Collection Number: 1–2–2]
  See the inventory at: https://rmc.library.cornell.edu/EAD/htmldocs/ RMA00002.html.
  NB: Most of White's papers are available on-line in the form of digitized PDFs of 148 microfilms: https://ecommons.cornell.edu/handle/1813/ 43964. Unfortunately, these are organized differently from the physical originals and they also include items from other collections. In fact, the entirety of White's correspondence with Burr can be found amongst George Lincoln Burr's papers (on which, see below). As I have consulted part of the letters in person and part digitally, I have decided to reference them solely by place and date but they can be retrieved using the link above and the following (digitized) inventory: Herb Finch, *Andrew Dickson White Papers at Cornell University, 1846–1919* (Ithaca, NY: Collection of Regional History and University Archives, 1970). https:// hdl.handle.net/1813/44116.
  George Lincoln Burr papers, 1861–1942 [Collection Number: 14–17–22]
  See the inventory at: https://rmc.library.cornell.edu/EAD/htmldocs/ RMA00022.html.

Oxford, Bodleian Library
  MS Bryce USA 12.

Philadelphia, University of Pennsylvania
  MS Coll. 111: Henry Charles Lea papers, Box 4, Folders 207–9.

Publications by Andrew Dickson White (Sorted Chronologically)

'Glimpses of Universal History'. *The New Englander*, 15 (1857), 398–427.
Outlines of a Course of Lectures on History, Addressed to the Senior Class (Detroit: H. Barns & Co., 1861).
'Jefferson and Slavery', *The Atlantic Monthly*, 9 (January 1862), 29–40.

'The Statesmanship of Richelieu', *The Atlantic Monthly*, 9 (May 1862), 611–24.

'The Development and Overthrow of the Russian Serf-System', *The Atlantic Monthly*, 10 (November 1862), 539–52.

'The American Institute: First of the Course of Scientific Lectures; Prof. White on "The Battle-Fields of Science"', *New York Daily Tribune*, 18 December 1869.

Outlines of a Course of Lectures on History, Addressed to the Senior Class (Ithaca, NY: The University Press, 1870).

Report Submitted to the Trustees of Cornell University, [on] Behalf of a Majority of the Committee on Mr Sage's Proposal to Endow a College for Women (Ithaca, NY: The University Press, 1872).

The Warfare of Science. London: Henry S. King & Co., 1876.

'The New Germany', *Journal of the American Geographical Society of New York*, 14 (1882), 205–58. https://doi.org/10.2307/196474.

'*What Profession Shall I Choose and How Shall I Fit Myself or It?' With a Brief Statement of Facilities Offered at the Cornell University* (Ithaca, NY: s.n., 1884).

Some Practical Influences of German Thought upon the United States (Ithaca, NY: Andrus & Church, 1884).

'On Studies in General History and the History of Civilization', *Papers of the American Historical Association*, 1, no. 2 (1885), 49–72.

Evolution and Revolution: An Address Delivered at the Annual Commencement of the University of Michigan, June 26, 1890 (Ann Arbor, MI: University of Michigan, 1890).

A History of the Warfare of Science with Theology in Christendom, 2 vols. (New York: D. Appleton and Co., 1896).

Proceedings at the Laying of a Wreath on the Tomb of Hugo Grotius in the Nieuwe Kerk, in the City of Delft (The Hague: M. Nijhoff, 1899).

Autobiography of Andrew Dickson White, 2 vols. (New York: The Century Co., 1905).

Seven Great Statesmen in the Warfare of Humanity with Unreason (New York: The Century Co., 1910).

Publications by George Lincoln Burr (Sorted Chronologically)

NB: Many of Burr's publications were assembled (often incorporating later hand-written corrections), together with a short biography by Roland H. Bainton, in:

Lois Oliphant Gibbons (ed.), *George Lincoln Burr: His Life [and] Selections from His Writings*, Ithaca, NY: Cornell University Press, 1943.

This volume is abbreviated below as Gibbons (ed.), *Burr* in the entries below, with the original year of publication of the item in brackets [].

'On the Loos Manuscript' [1886], in Gibbons (ed.), *Burr*, pp. 147–55.

'The Literature of Witchcraft' [1889] in Gibbons (ed.), *Burr*, pp. 166–89.

'The Fate of Dietrich Flade' [1890] in Gibbons (ed.), *Burr*, pp. 190–233.

'The Living Gospel' [1891] in Gibbons (ed.), *Burr*, pp. 234–42.

'Sketch of Andrew Dickson White', *Popular Science Monthly*, February 1896, 546–56.

(ed.), *The Witch-Persecutions*, Translations and Reprints from the Original Sources of European History (Philadelphia: The Department of History of the University of Pennsylvania, 1897).

'A Witch-Hunter in the Book-Shops' [1902] in Gibbons (ed.), *Burr*, pp. 294–308.

'Religious Progress' [1905] in Gibbons (ed.), *Burr*, 309–15.

'New England's Place in the History of Witchcraft' [1911] in Gibbons (ed.), *Burr*, pp. 352–77.

'Andrew Dickson White' [1918] in Gibbons (ed.), *Burr*, pp. 415–19.

'Review of *Review of The Witch-Cult in Western Europe: A Study in Anthropology*, by Margaret Alice Murray', *The American Historical Review*, 27, no. 4 (1922), 780–83. https://doi.org/10.2307/1837549.

'A Group of Four Books on Witchcraft and Demonology' [1928] in Gibbons (ed.), *Burr*, pp. 491–95.

'Review of "Witchcraft in Old and New England"; By George Lyman Kittredge, Gurney Professor of English Literature in Harvard University', *American Historical Review*, 34, no. 4 (1929), 814–17. https://doi.org/10.1086/ahr/34.4.814.

'Introduction to Lea's Materials toward a History of Witchcraft' [1938] in Gibbons (ed.), *Burr*, pp. 454–74.

Other Pre-1900 Publications

Adams, Charles Kendall, 'A Manuscript and a Man', *The Nation*, 11 November 1886.

Boulton, Richard, *A Compleat History of Magick, Sorcery, and Witchcraft* (London: E. Curll, J. Pemberton, and W. Taylor, 1715).

Delrio, Martin, *Disquisitionum magicarum libri sex in tres tomos partiti*, 3 vols. (Mainz: Johannes Albinus, 1603).

Draper, John William, *History of the Conflict Between Religion and Science* (New York: D. Appleton and Company, 1875).

Glover, A. Kingsley, 'Rome and the Inquisitions', *The North American Review*, 141, no. 349 (1885), 533–39.

Hutchinson, Francis, *An Historical Essay Concerning Witchcraft: With Observations upon Matters of Fact; Tending to Clear the Texts of the Sacred Scriptures and Confute the Vulgar Errors about That Point* (London: R. Knaplock and D. Midwinter, 1718).

Scott, Sir Walter, *Letters on Demonology and Witchcraft Addressed to J. G. Lockhart, Esq.* (London: John Murray, 1830).

Thomasius, Christian, *Disputatio iuris canonici de origine ac progressu processus inquisitorii contra sagas* (Halle: Johann Christoph Krebs, 1712).

Publications Post-1900

Alberti, Johanna, *Gender and the Historian* (Harlow: Longman, 2002).

Almond, Philip C., *England's First Demonologist Reginald Scot and 'The Discoverie of Witchcraft'* (London: I. B. Tauris, 2011).

Almond, Philip C., 'You Think This Is a Witch Hunt, Mr President? That's an Insult to the Women Who Suffered', *The Conversation*, 20 January 2020. http://theconversation.com/you-think-this-is-a-witch-hunt-mr-president-thats-an-insult-to-the-women-who-suffered-129775.

Altschuler, Glenn C., *Andrew D. White, Educator, Historian, Diplomat* (Ithaca, NY: Cornell University Press, 1979).

Apps, Lara, and Andrew Colin Gow, *Male Witches in Early Modern Europe* (Manchester: Manchester University Press, 2003).

Bainton, Roland H. 'His Life' in Lois Oliphant Gibbons (ed.), *George Lincoln Burr: His Life and Selections from His Writings* (Ithaca: Cornell University Press, 1943), pp. 3–143.

Beach, Mark B., 'Andrew Dickson White as Ex-President: The Plight of a Retired Reformer', *American Quarterly*, 17, no. 2 (1965), 239–47. https://doi.org/10.2307/2711357.

Behringer, Wolfgang, 'Germany' in Richard M. Golden (ed.), *Encyclopedia of Witchcraft: The Western Tradition* (Santa Barbara: ABC-CLIO, 2006), vol. II, pp. 416–17.

Behringer, Wolfgang, 'Neun Millionen Hexen: Entstehung, Tradition und Kritik eines poplären Mythos', *Geschichte in Wissenschaft und Unterricht* 49, no. 11 (1998), 664–85.

Behringer, Wolfgang, 'Witchcraft Studies in Austria, Germany and Switzerland' in Jonathan Barry, Marianne Hester, and Gareth Roberts (eds.), *Witchcraft in Early Modern Europe: Studies in Culture and Belief* (Cambridge: Cambridge University Press, 1996), pp. 64–95.

Bordin, Ruth, *Andrew Dickson White, Teacher of History* (Ann Arbor: The University of Michigan, 1958).

Bostridge, Ian, *Witchcraft and Its Transformations, c.1650–c.1750* (Oxford: Clarendon Press, 1997).

Brooke, John Hedley, *Science and Religion: Some Historical Perspectives* (Cambridge: Cambridge University Press, 1991).

Cameron, Euan, *Enchanted Europe: Superstition, Reason, and Religion, 1250–1750* (Oxford: Oxford University Press, 2010).

'Centenary of Birth of Dr. Andrew White Celebrated by Alumni', *Cornell Daily Sun*, 12 November 1932.

Clark, Stuart, *Thinking with Demons: The Idea of Witchcraft in Early Modern Europe* (Oxford: Clarendon Press, 1997).

Clark, William, *Academic Charisma and the Origins of the Research University* (Chicago: University of Chicago Press, 2006).

Cohn, Norman, *Europe's Inner Demons: An Enquiry Inspired by the Great Witch-Hunt* (London: Chatto & Windus, 1975).

Daly, Mary, *Gyn/Ecology* (London: The Women's Press, 1979).

Daston, Lorraine and H. Otto Sibum, 'Introduction: Scientific Personae and Their Histories', *Science in Context*, 16, no. 1–2 (2003), 1-8. https://doi.org /10.1017/S026988970300067X.

Davies, Owen, and Willem de Blécourt (eds.), *Witchcraft Continued: Popular Magic in Modern Europe* (Manchester: Manchester University Press, 2004).

Davis, Natalie Zemon, 'Gender and Genre: Women as Historical Writers, 1400-1820' in Patricia H. Labalme (ed.), *Beyond Their Sex: Learned Women of the European Past* (New York: New York University Press, 1980), pp. 153–82.

Dixon, Thomas, *Science and Religion: A Very Short Introduction* (Oxford: Oxford University Press, 2008).

'Dr A.D. White dies: A Cornell Founder', *New York Times*, 5 November 1918.

Epple, Angelika, 'Historiographiegeschichte als Diskursanalyse und Analytik der Macht: eine Neubestimmung der Geschichtsschreibung unter den Bedingungen der Geschlechtergeschichte', *L'Homme: Zeitschrift für Feministische Geschichtswissenschaft*, 15, no. 1 (2004), 67–86. https://doi .org/10.25595/1045.

Epple, Angelika, and Angelika Schaser (eds.), *Gendering Historiography: Beyond National Canons* (Frankfurt: Campus Verlag, 2009).

Estes, Leland L., 'Incarnations of Evil: Changing Perspectives on the European Witch Craze', *Clio* 13, no. 2 (1984), 133–47.

'Excerpt from Prof. Burr's Speech', *Cornell Daily Sun*, 12 November 1932.

Falk, Seb, *The Light Ages: A Medieval Journey of Discovery* (London: Allen Lane, 2020).

Fels, Tony, *Switching Sides: How a Generation of Historians Lost Sympathy for the Victims of the Salem Witch Hunt* (Baltimore: Johns Hopkins University Press, 2018).

Ferngren, Gary B., *Science and Religion: A Historical Introduction* (Baltimore: Johns Hopkins University Press, 2002).

Franz, Gunther, 'Antonius Hovaeus, Cornelius Loos und Friedrich Spee: Drei Gegner der Hexenprozesse in Echternach und Trier' in Gunther Franz, Günter Gehl, and Franz Irsigler (eds.), *Hexenprozesse und deren Gegner im Trierisch-Lothringischen Raum* (Weimar: Dadder, 1997), pp. 117–42.

Fudge, Thomas A., 'Traditions and Trajectories in the Historiography of European Witch Hunting', *History Compass*, 4, no. 3 (2006), 488–527. https://doi.org/10.1111/j.1478-0542.2006.00310.x.

Gaskill, Malcolm, 'The Pursuit of Reality: Recent Research into the History of Witchcraft', *The Historical Journal*, 51, no. 4 (2008), 1069–99. https://doi.org/10.1017/S0018246X0800719X.

Gibson, Marion, *Witchcraft Myths in American Culture* (London: Routledge, 2007).

Guerlac, Henry, 'George Lincoln Burr', *Isis*, 35, no. 2 (1944), 147–52. https://doi.org/10.1086/358686.

Guskin, Phyllis J., 'The Context of Witchcraft: The Case of Jane Wenham (1712)', *Eighteenth-Century Studies*, 15, no. 1 (1981), 48–71. https://doi.org/10.2307/2738402.

Haines, Patricia Foster, 'For Honor and Alma Mater: Perspectives on Coeducation at Cornell University, 1868–1885', *The Journal of Education*, 159, no. 3 (1977), 25–37. https://doi.org/10.1177/002205747615900305.

Harrison, Peter, 'Myth 24: That Religion Has Typically Impeded the Progress of Science' in Ronald L. Numbers and Kostas Kampourakis (eds.), *Newton's Apple and Other Myths about Science* (Cambridge, MA: Harvard University Press, 2015), pp. 195–201.

Harrison, Peter, *The Territories of Science and Religion* (Chicago: University of Chicago Press, 2015).

Hawkins, Mike, *Social Darwinism in European and American Thought, 1860–1945: Nature as Model and Nature as Threat* (Cambridge: Cambridge University Press, 1997).

Hewett, Waterman Thomas, *Cornell University: A History*, 4 vols. (New York: The University Publishing Society, 1905).

Hoorens, Vera, *Een ketterse arts voor de heksen: Jan Wier, 1515–1588* (Amsterdam: Bakker, 2011).

Hunter, Michael, *The Decline of Magic: Britain in the Enlightenment* (New Haven: Yale University Press, 2020).

Hutton, Ronald, *The Triumph of the Moon: A History of Modern Pagan Witchcraft* (Oxford: Oxford University Press, 1999).

Hutton, Ronald, *The Witch: A History of Fear, from Ancient Times to the Present* (New Haven: Yale University Press, 2017).

Iggers, Georg G., 'The Image of Ranke in American and German Historical Thought', *History and Theory* 2, no. 1 (1962), 17–40. https://doi.org/10.2307/2504333.

Iggers, Georg G., The Intellectual Foundations of Nineteenth-Century "Scientific" History: The German Model' in Stuart Macintyre, Juan Maiguashca, and Attila Pók (eds.), *The Oxford History of Historical Writing*, vol. IV: 1800–1945 (Oxford: Oxford University Press), pp. 41–57.

Institoris, Heinrich, and Jakob Sprenger, *Malleus Maleficarum: The Hammer of Witches*, ed. and trans. Christopher S. Mackay, 2 vols. (Cambridge: Cambridge University Press, 2006).

Johnstone, Nathan, *The New Atheism, Myth, and History: The Black Legends of Contemporary Anti-Religion* (Basingstoke: Palgrave Macmillan, 2018).

Kauertz, Claudia, *Wissenschaft und Hexenglaube: Die Diskussion des Zauber- und Hexenwesens an der Universität Helmstedt, 1576–1626* (Bielefeld: Verlag für Regionalgeschichte, 2001).

Kemper, Dietmar, 'Frank Sobiech Erhält den Preis des Paderborner Geschichtsvereins: Friedrich Spee und die Hexen', *Westfalen-Blatt*, 10 December 2019.

Kimmel, Michael, *Manhood in America: A Cultural History* (New York: Free Press, 1996).

Kittredge, George Lyman, *Notes on Witchcraft* (Worcester, MA: The Davis Press, 1907).

Levack, Brian P., 'Crime and the Law' in Jonathan Barry and Owen Davies (eds.), *Palgrave Advances in Witchcraft Historiography* (Basingstoke: Palgrave Macmillan, 2007), pp. 146–63.

Lindberg, David C., and Ronald L. Numbers, 'Beyond War and Peace: A Reappraisal of the Encounter between Christianity and Science', *Church History*, 55, no. 3 (1986), 338–54. https://doi.org/10.2307/3166822.

Lingelbach, Gabriele, 'The Institutionalization and Professionalization of History in Europe and the United States' in Stuart Macintyre, Juan Maiguashca, and Attila Pók (eds.), *The Oxford History of Historical Writing*, vol. IV: 1800–1945 (Oxford: Oxford University Press), pp. 78–96.

Livio, Mario, *Galileo and the Science Deniers* (New York: Simon & Schuster, 2020).

Lowenthal, David, *The Past Is a Foreign Country – Revisited*, rev. ed. (Cambridge: Cambridge University Press, 2015).

Machielsen, Jan, *Martin Delrio: Demonology and Scholarship in the Counter-Reformation* (Oxford: Oxford University Press, 2015).

Machielsen, Jan, 'Review of "The Decline of Magic: Britain in the Enlightenment"', *Reviews in History*, no. 2393 (2000). https://reviews.history.ac.uk/review/2393.

Malkiel, Nancy Weiss, *"Keep the Damned Women Out": The Struggle for Coeducation* (Princeton: Princeton University Press, 2016).

Meyer, Thomas Hilarius, 'Systematische Theologie, katechetische Strenge und pädagogisches Augenmaß: Die Tübinger Theologen und die Hexenverfolgungen am Beispiel Jakob Heerbrands' in Ulrich Köpf, Sönke Lorenz, and Dieter R. Bauer (eds.), *Die Universität Tübingen zwischen Reformation und Dreißigjährigem Krieg* (Ostfildern: Jan Thorbecke, 2010), pp. 165–80.

Miller, Arthur, 'Why I Wrote "The Crucible"', *The New Yorker*, 14 October 1996.

Monter, E. William, 'The Historiography of European Witchcraft: Progress and Prospects', *The Journal of Interdisciplinary History*, 2, no. 4 (1972), 435–51. https://doi.org/10.2307/202315.

Murray, Margaret Alice, *My First Hundred Years* (London: William Kimber, 1963).

Notestein, Wallace, *A History of Witchcraft in England from 1558 to 1718* (Washington: The American Historical Association, 1911).

Novick, Peter, *That Noble Dream: The 'Objectivity Question' and the American Historical Profession* (Cambridge: Cambridge University Press, 1988).

Numbers, Ronald L. (ed.), *Galileo Goes to Jail and Other Myths about Science and Religion* (Cambridge, MA: Harvard University Press, 2009).

Numbers, Ronald L., and Kostas Kampourakis (eds.), *Newton's Apple and Other Myths about Science* (Cambridge, MA: Harvard University Press, 2015).

Nuttall, A. D., *Dead from the Waist Down: Scholars and Scholarship in Literature and the Popular Imagination* (New Haven: Yale University Press, 2003).

Oates, Caroline, *A Coven of Scholars: Margaret Murray and Her Working Methods* (London: Folklore Society, 1998).

Ogden, Robert Morris (ed.), *The Diaries of Andrew D. White* (Ithaca: Cornell University Library, 1959).

Park, Katharine, 'That the Medieval Church Prohibited Human Dissection' in Ronald L. Numbers (ed.), *Galileo Goes to Jail and Other Myths about Science and Religion* (Cambridge, MA: Harvard University Press, 2009), pp. 43–9.

Paul, Herman, 'What Is a Scholarly Persona? Ten Theses on Virtues, Skills, and Desires', *History and Theory* 53 (2014), 348–71. https://doi.org/10.1111/hith .10717.

Persecution and Liberty: Essays in Honor of George Lincoln Burr (New York: The Century Co., 1931).

Pooley, William. 'Magical Capital: Witchcraft and the Press in Paris, c. 1789–1939' in Karl Bell (ed.), *Supernatural Cities: Enchantment, Anxiety and Spectrality* (Woodbridge: The Boydell Press, 2019), pp. 25–44.

Pooley, William, 'Review of "The Decline of Magic: Britain in the Enlightenment" by Michael Hunter', *Folklore*, 131, no. 4 (2020), 443–5. https://doi.org/10.1080/0015587X.2020.1827834.

Purkiss, Diane, *The Witch in History: Early Modern and Twentieth-Century Representations* (London: Routledge, 1996).

'Retires in February: G. L. Burr', *The Cornell Daily Sun*, 20 January 1922.

Robbins, Rossell Hope, *Witchcraft: An Introduction to the Literature of Witchcraft, Being the Preface and Introduction to the Catalogue of the Witchcraft Collection in Cornell University Library* (Millwood: KTO Press, 1978).

Roper, Lyndal, *Oedipus and the Devil: Witchcraft, Sexuality and Religion in Early Modern Europe* (London: Routledge, 1994).

Rosen, Edward, 'Calvin's Attitude Toward Copernicus', *Journal of the History of Ideas*, 21, no. 3 (1960), 431–41. https://doi.org/10.2307/2708147.

Ross, Dorothy, 'On the Misunderstanding of Ranke and the Origins of the Historical Profession in America', in Georg G. Iggers and James M. Powell (eds.), *Leopold von Ranke and the Shaping of the Historical Discipline* (Syracuse: Syracuse University Press, 1990), pp. 154–69.

Rowlands, Alison (ed.), *Witchcraft and Masculinities in Early Modern Europe* (Basingstoke: Palgrave Macmillan, 2009).

Rublack, Ulinka, *The Astronomer and the Witch: Johannes Kepler's Fight for his Mother* (Oxford: Oxford University Press, 2015).

Russell, Colin A., 'The Conflict of Science and Religion' in Gary B Ferngren (ed.), *Science and Religion: A Historical Introduction* (Baltimore: Johns Hopkins University Press, 2002), pp. 3–12.

Russell, Jeffrey Burton, *Inventing the Flat Earth: Columbus and Modern Historians* (New York: Praeger, 1991).

Schaefer, Richard. 'Andrew Dickson White and the History of a Religious Future', *Zygon*, 50, no. 1 (2015), 7–27. https://doi.org/10.1111/zygo.12148.

Schiffman, Zachary, *The Birth of the Past* (Baltimore: Johns Hopkins University Press, 2011).

Schnicke, Falko, *Die männliche Disziplin: Zur Vergeschlechtlichung der deutschen Geschichtswissenschaft 1780–1900* (Göttingen: Wallstein Verlag, 2015).

Scholer, Othon, '"O Kehricht Des Aberglaubens, o Leerer Wahn Der Täuschungen Und Gespenster Der Nacht!": Der Angriff Des Cornelius Loos Auf Petrus Binsfeld' in Gunther Franz and Franz Irsigler (eds.), *Methoden und Konzepte der Historischen Hexenforschung* (Trier: Spee, 1998), pp. 255–76.

Schulte, Rolf, *Man as Witch: Male Witches in Central Europe* (Basingstoke: Palgrave Macmillan, 2009).

Scott, Joan Wallach, *Gender and the Politics of History*, rev. ed. (New York: Columbia University Press, 1999).

Shuck, Glenn William, 'The Myth of the Burning Times and the Politics of Resistance in Contemporary American Wicca', *Journal of Religion and Society*, 2 (2000), 1–9.

Simpson, Jacqueline, 'Margaret Murray: Who Believed Her, and Why?', *Folklore*, 105, no. 1/2 (1994), 89–96. https://doi.org/10.1080/0015587x.1994.9715877.

Sisman, Adam, *Hugh Trevor-Roper: The Biography* (London: Weidenfeld & Nicolson, 2010).

Smith, Bonnie G., 'Gender and the Practices of Scientific History: The Seminar and Archival Research in the Nineteenth Century', *The American Historical Review*, 100, no. 4 (1995), 1150–76. https://doi.org/10.2307/2168205.

Smith, Bonnie G., *The Gender of History: Men, Women, and Historical Practice* (Cambridge, MA: Harvard University Press, 1998).

Smith, S. A. 'Introduction' in S. A. Smith (ed.), *The Religion of Fools? Superstition, Past and Present*, Past and Present Supplement 3 (2008), 7–55. https://doi.org/10.1093/pastj/gtm058.

Sneddon, Andrew, *Witchcraft and Whigs: The Life of Bishop Francis Hutchinson (1660–1739)* (Manchester: Manchester University Press, 2008).

Sobiech, Frank, *Jesuit Prison Ministry in the Witch Trials of the Holy Roman Empire: Friedrich Spee SJ and His Cautio Criminalis (1631)* (Rome: Institutum Historicum Societatis Iesu, 2019).

Summers, Montague, *The Galanty Show: An Autobiography* (London: C. Woolf, 1980).

Summers, Montague, *The History of Witchcraft and Demonology* (London: Kegan Paul, 1926).

'The Cornell University Witchcraft Collection'. https://rmc.library.cornell.edu /witchcraftcoll/index.php.

'The Witch Hunter', *Essex Newsman*, 27 February 1945.

Thomas, Keith. *Religion and the Decline of Magic: Studies in Popular Beliefs in Sixteenth- and Seventeenth-Century England* (London: Weidenfeld & Nicolson, 1971).

Trevor-Roper, Hugh R. 'The European Witch-Craze of the Sixteenth and Seventeenth Centuries' in *The Crisis of the Seventeenth Century: Religion, the Reformation and Social Change* (Indianapolis: Liberty Fund, 2001 [1969]), pp. 83–178.

Tuczay, Christa, 'The Nineteenth Century: Medievalism and Witchcraft' in Jonathan Barry and Owen Davies (eds.), *Palgrave Advances in Witchcraft Historiography* (Basingstoke: Palgrave Macmillan, 2007), pp. 52–68.

Turner, Frederick Jackson, *The Frontier in American History* (New York: H. Holt and Company, 1920).

Ungureanu, James C., 'Science and Religion in the Anglo-American Periodical Press, 1860–1900: A Failed Reconciliation', *Church History*, 88, no. 1 (2019), 120–49. https://doi.org/10.1017/S0009640719000532.

Valente, Michaela, *Johann Wier: Agli albori della critica razionale dell'occulto e del demoniaco nell'Europa del Cinquecento* (Florence: L. S. Olschki, 2003).

Van der Eerden, P.C., 'Der Teufelspakt bei Binsfeld und Loos' in Gunther Franz and Franz Irsigler (eds.), *Hexenglaube und Hexenprozesse im Raum Rhein-Mosel-Saar* (Trier: Spee, 1995), pp. 51–72.

Voltmer, Rita, 'Demonology and Anti-Demonology: Binsfeld's De confessionibus and Loos's De vera et falsa magia' in Jan Machielsen (ed.), *The Science of Demons: Early Modern Authors Facing Witchcraft and the Devil* (London: Routledge, 2020), pp. 149–64.

Voltmer, Rita, 'Ein Amerikaner in Trier: George Lincoln Burr (1857-1938) und sein Beitrag zu den Sammelschwerpunkten "Hexerei und Hexenverfolgungen" an der Cornell University (Ithaca/New York) sowie an der Stadtbibliothek Trier; mit einem Inventar', *Kurtrierisches Jahrbuch*, 47 (2007), 447–89.

Voltmer, Rita 'Flade, Dietrich (1534-1589)' in Richard M. Golden (ed.), *Encyclopedia of Witchcraft: The Western Tradition* (Santa Barbara: ABC-CLIO, 2006), vol. II, pp. 378–9.

Voltmer, Rita, '"Germany's First 'Superhunt'?" Rezeption und Konstruktion der so genannten Trierer Verfolgungen (16.–21. Jahrhundert)' in

Katrin Moeller and Burghart Schmidt (eds.), *Realität und Mythos: Hexenverfolgung und Rezeptionsgeschichte* (Hamburg: DOBU Verlag, 2003), pp. 225–58.

Voltmer, Rita. 'Loos, Cornelius (1540 to 1546-1596?)' in Richard M. Golden (ed.), *Encyclopedia of Witchcraft: The Western Tradition* (Santa Barbara: ABC-CLIO, 2006), vol. III, pp. 666–7.

Voltmer, Rita, 'Witch-Finders, Witch-Hunters or Kings of the Sabbath? The Prominent Role of Men in the Mass Persecutions of the Rhine-Meuse Area (Sixteenth-Seventeenth Centuries)' in Alison Rowlands (ed.), *Witchcraft and Masculinities in Early Modern Europe* (Basingstoke: Palgrave Macmillan, 2009), pp. 74–99.

Walker, Garthine. 'Modernization' in Garthine Walker (ed.), *Writing Early Modern History* (London: Hodder Arnold, 2005), pp. 25–48.

Walsham, Alexandra, 'The Reformation and "the Disenchantment of the World" Reassessed', *The Historical Journal*, 51, no. 2 (2008), 497–528. https://doi.org/10.1017/S0018246X08006808.

Waters, Thomas, *Cursed Britain: A History of Witchcraft and Black Magic in Modern Times* (New Haven: Yale University Press, 2019).

Welch, Evelyn, 'Presentism and the Renaissance and Early Modern Historian', *Past and Present*, 234, no. 1 (2017), 245–53. https://doi.org/10.1093/pastj/gtw058.

Werner, Anja, *The Transatlantic World of Higher Education: Americans at German Universities, 1776–1914* (New York: Berghahn Books, 2013).

Whitney, Elspeth, 'The Witch "She"/The Historian "He": Gender and the Historiography of the European Witch-Hunts', *Journal of Women's History*, 7, no. 3 (1995), 77–101. https://doi.org/10.1353/jowh.2010.0511.

Willis, Deborah, *Malevolent Nurture: Witch-Hunting and Maternal Power in Early Modern England* (Ithaca: Cornell University Press, 1995).

Wood, Juliette, 'The Reality of Witch Cults Reasserted: Fertility and Satanism' in Jonathan Barry and Owen Davies (eds.), *Palgrave Advances in Witchcraft Historiography* (Basingstoke: Palgrave Macmillan, 2007), pp. 69–89.

Acknowledgements

This Element was a long time in the making and – perhaps inevitably, given its subject matter – its debts are so many they cannot and should not be contained in a footnote. Its origins go back to 2010 when, as a graduate student, I was the recipient of a scholarship to Cornell University from the Abraham and Henrietta Brettschneider Oxford Exchange Fund, which provided me with an opportunity to study its large witchcraft collection. Sydney Van Morgan and Lianne O'Brien were excellent hosts at Cornell's Institute for European Studies, as was Duane Corpis at Cornell's History Department. It was an honour to be invited to present a seminar paper at Andrew Dickson White House, although I did not quite appreciate the significance of the place at the time. It was as a result of working on Cornell's many witchcraft holdings that I became interested in the collection's origins, and a grant from my then Oxford college, New College, enabled my return in 2014. I am grateful to Laurent Ferri for his hospitality during that visit, although I suspect our views on Burr, in particular, may differ.

A first version of this text began life as a long article in 2016. Its position at the intersection between a great many different fields of scholarship – so much so that it might resemble Swindon's Magic Roundabout – has also entailed many debts and I am grateful to the many experts – on history of witchcraft, science, scholarship, historiography, masculinity, and America – who cast their light on drafts of this text. In particular, I would like to thank David Doddington, Malcolm Gaskill, Anthony Grafton, Peter Harrison, Hannah Murphy, Johan Olsthoorn, Anthony Ossa Richardson, Alison Rowlands, Lyndal Roper, and Rita Voltmer for their thoughts and comments. I wish I could be equally thankful to any of the three leading academic journals that each on average took a year to reject the original article version of this text, or to the reviewers who sought to damn it with faint praise ('it's true subject is ... the history of Cornell') or denounce it for 'playing to current fads in the academy'. I am therefore exceptionally grateful to Marion Gibson and Alex Wright at Cambridge University Press for encouraging me to expand the argument into an Element and accepting it in the series. For once, Reviewer Two was also an absolute wonder of constructive and helpful feedback. White and Burr would, at different times in their lives, have been either delighted or horrified that this rewrite took place during a research stay in Germany funded by the Humboldt foundation. I would like to thank Gerd Schwerhoff for being an exceptional mentor and host at the TU Dresden during the challenging circumstances of a pandemic.

In terms of silver linings, the delay in publication gave me the opportunity to supervise a number of undergraduate dissertations on witchcraft historiography. Jack Maynard, Rebecca Parkes, and Robert Pearce all taught me things about the origins of my own field that I did not know. The Covid lockdown, for all its difficulties, provided an opportunity for Will Pooley and me to organize two highly successful Zoom workshops on the theme of the decline of magic. I want to thank Will and the many other participants, including Helen Cornish, Kristof Smeyers (who told me about the Thomasius engraving), and Thomas Waters, for their comments and their own stimulating papers. Thanks are also due to Eisha Neely and Evan Earle at Cornell University Library and Maria Smit at the Rijksmuseum, Amsterdam, for their help with the images and image rights. Finally, I want to record my heartfelt gratitude to two friends, Hannah Murphy and Anthony Ossa Richardson, who each in their own way have supported this project (and its author) through its many ups and downs, providing much needed encouragement on the downhill slopes. From the outset Anthony felt that this Element should be a book. To the extent that it is, it is dedicated to him.

Cambridge Elements ≡

Magic

Marion Gibson
University of Exeter

Marion Gibson is Professor of Renaissance and Magical Literatures and Director of the Flexible Combined Honours Programme at the University of Exeter. Her publications include *Possession, Puritanism and Print: Darrell, Harsnett, Shakespeare and the Elizabethan Exorcism Controversy* (2006), *Witchcraft Myths in American Culture* (2007), *Imagining the Pagan Past: Gods and Goddesses in Literature and History since the Dark Ages* (2013), *The Arden Shakespeare Dictionary of Shakespeare's Demonology* (with Jo Esra, 2014), *Rediscovering Renaissance Witchcraft* (2017) and *Witchcraft: The Basics* (2018). Her new book, *The Witches of St Osyth: Persecution, Murder and Betrayal in Elizabethan England*, will be published by CUP in 2022.

About the Series

Elements in Magic aims to restore the study of magic, broadly defined, to a central place within culture: one which it occupied for many centuries before being set apart by changing discourses of rationality and meaning. Understood as a continuing and potent force within global civilisation, magical thinking is imaginatively approached here as a cluster of activities, attitudes, beliefs and motivations which include topics such as alchemy, astrology, divination, exorcism, the fantastical, folklore, haunting, supernatural creatures, necromancy, ritual, spirit possession and witchcraft.

Cambridge Elements ☰

Magic

Elements in the Series

The Strix-Witch
Daniel Ogden

*The War on Witchcraft: Andrew Dickson White, George Lincoln Burr, and the
Origins of Witchcraft Historiography*
Jan Machielsen

A full series listing is available at: www.cambridge.org/EMGI

Printed in the United States
by Baker & Taylor Publisher Services